Accidental Entrepreneur
Towards Self-Employment

Accidental Entrepreneur

Towards Self-Employment

Puneet Srivastava

Rupa & Co

Published 2004 by

Rupa & Co

7/16, Ansari Road, Daryaganj,
New Delhi 110 002

Sales Centres:

Allahabad Bangalore Chandigarh Chennai
Hyderabad Jaipur Kathmandu
Kolkata Ludhiana Mumbai Pune

Typeset in 11 pts. Classical Garamond by
Nikita Overseas Pvt Ltd,
1410 Chiranjiv Tower,
43 Nehru Place
New Delhi 110 019

Printed in India by
Gopsons Papers Ltd.,
A-14 Sector 60
Noida 201 301

You teach best what you most need to learn.

Richard Bach in *Illusions*

Contents

Preface

Unemployment and professional redundancy have been two major problems in our country for several decades now. Thousands of young people, armed with all kind of degrees and diplomas get pushed into the job market every year. Every year young professionals from all across the country flood all major commercial centres looking for a job. Unfortunately not everybody succeeds. Even among those who manage to find a job, several remain badly under-employed, doing something, which otherwise they might not have preferred to do in the first place.

The unemployment problem also has its links to the phenomenon of downsizing or what the 'reformists' prefer to call – 'right-sizing'. Over the last few years, almost all the big companies have been retrenching people as a means to cut costs and strengthen their bottom lines. With more people going out of the jobs than coming in, today we can find an entire brigade of qualified mid-career professionals sitting redundant, waiting for a suitable opening and wondering what to do next.

The question is—Can there be any practical solution to this long-standing and ever growing problem of unemployment?

A possible answer could be suggested in self-employment and entrepreneurship.

But then, entrepreneurship is not something which could be adopted easily by everybody. It is a career, which not only requires a specific kind of aptitude, but also a very different kind of a mindset. The question is that can these people, who have been out of job and likely to be running low on money and morale, dream to embrace successfully something as challenging as entrepreneurship? Can they acquire the necessary skills and the mindset needed for the job? In a profession where nearly two out of every three aspirants fail, what chance do such accidental entrepreneurs have of succeeding? In other words, can entrepreneurship, one of the highest manifestations of leadership in action, be nurtured among those who have been forced into an adverse situation called unemployment?

I feel *Yes*, entrepreneurship can be nurtured and that is what this book is all about. *Accidental Entrepreneur* is a book for people who would want to take to self-employment to get rid of unemployment. It has been written with an objective to help fellow-professionals understand the tricks of the trade and encourage them to see self-employment as a viable career option.

Someone once asked Lee Kuan Yew, the Senior Minister of Singapore, the same old question: "Are leaders born or made?" Lee Kuan Yew answered, "Leaders can be made, provided they are born!"

I feel the same holds true for entrepreneurs. Entrepreneurs can be made, provided they are born. Incidentally, most of us have the potential to be an entrepreneur. But only very few of us attempt to utilize this hidden potential.

Further, I can speak from my own experience and can confirm for sure that entrepreneurship can be nurtured. Only till a few years back I was an educationally qualified, willing to work and yet an unemployed professional. Then one day, after losing all the hopes of finding a proper job, I decided to try my hand at self-employment. It has taken me five years and three failed attempts to get to where I am today, a Freelance Marketing Consultant, busy running a growing business and earning a decent living. I am what you can rightly call – An Accidental Entrepreneur.

So if I can, why not you or anyone, who tries!

There are two ways of learning anything – the hard way and the smart way. I had to learn things the *hard way*, because I could not at that point of time visualize any other option. But here in this book I shall share with you several tricks that would help you learn and implement things the smart way.

Before we move any further, I feel it is highly important to understand the difference between the two terms that we have been using almost interchangeably. These are:

1. Self-employment
2. Entrepreneurship

The question is—Are they synonyms? If not, then why are they being used interchangeably?

To begin with the definitions, while 'Self-employment' is largely about earning a living by being on your own, 'Entrepreneurship' is about working to make a DREAM come true...some day. For example, being a teacher and taking private tuitions is self-employment, while aspiring to build an educational institute is entrepreneurship.

Entrepreneurship is nothing but an enlarged/magnified version of self-employment. Both require similar fundamentals for success. Interestingly self-employment can serve as an ideal launch pad for becoming a full-fledged entrepreneur. Something several others have done in the past and something every accidental entrepreneur can aspire to do! Anyhow throughout this book both these terms would be used more as concepts rather than in reference to the individual meanings they might convey and thus would be used interchangeably.

It might sound strange to some, but the truth remains that more than 60 per cent of all entrepreneurial ventures fail within five years of their inception. I too have been party to three failures. Thankfully, none of them were big or fatal enough to prevent me from moving forward. Over these years, one question that has always bothered me has been:

Despite all the enthusiasm and commitment shown on part of the individual entrepreneurs, why do entrepreneurial ventures fail in such numbers? Can't something be done to arrest, if not totally prevent these failures?

Experts say that failure is an integral part of the process of evolving as an entrepreneur. However that does not mean that we should look forward to embrace failures. Entrepreneurial failures could be catastrophic and should be avoided at every cost.

Accordingly, the second objective of this book is to help self-employed professionals and entrepreneurs avoid failures and embrace survival, if not immediate success.

Please remember that survival is a pre-requisite for success and to witness repeated success one must keep surviving still longer.

This is largely a self-help book where all the aspects of entrepreneurship have been covered in a step-by-step manner. Interestingly the relationship between an entrepreneur and his/her venture is very similar to the one shared between a mother and her child. Both render massive influence on each other. It would be meaningless to talk about one without making any reference to the other, in fact it is impossible.

Even in this book, we shall on several occasions, make quick transition between the two domains without any specific warnings. It is because the two are practically inseparable and must be talked about in conjunction to make any sense. Some readers might find this practice a little different from the way proceedings in other streams of Business Management are normally documented. When talking about Business Management as a subject, we talk about two things, 'the business' and 'the people running that business', separately. However, that is not possible in case of an entrepreneurial set-up; the entrepreneur and his/her venture are inseparable and have to be discussed simultaneously.

To get the ball rolling, every entrepreneurial journey can be distinctly divided into four interconnected phases. These are:

1. Getting Ready Phase
2. Planning Phase
3. Implementation Phase
4. Audit Phase

Every entrepreneur has to go through all these four phases before he/she can be labeled successful in any way. Interestingly, continued success only means going through the same cycle again and again. To put it differently, entrepreneurship is not like a 100-meter dash, where you win or lose in a matter of few seconds. Instead it is like a never-ending marathon, where the only way to win is to keep running. It is a race that goes endlessly round and round the racing track; the longer you run the bigger a winner you become.

Accordingly, the book has been divided into four sections, one each for every phase of the entrepreneurial cycle. There are three chapters in every section, each addressing one micro aspect relevant to that particular phase. The details are listed below:

Section I – Getting Ready Phase

1. Understanding the Basics
2. The Best Business to Start
3. The Best Time to Start

Section II – Planning Phase

4. Evolving the Plan
5. Designing the Road Map
6. Blocking the Loopholes

Section III – Implementation Phase

7. Creating an Identity
8. Staying in Cash
9. Leading and Networking

Section IV – Audit Phase

Finally, this is not a book that would tell the readers some magic formula to a quick million. In fact it might not even offer them any solutions, but where it shall definitely help them would be in identifying the critical areas and asking the right questions.

It must be understood that there are no ready-made solutions in offering for anything, anywhere. Any solutions we desire have to be derived by carefully identifying the problem; any answers we seek would have to be found by asking the right questions.

This book does not offer any instant solution; instead it is to motivate readers to ask questions, a lot of questions and still more questions... because questions are the only gateways to the answers we seek.

To put it in a nutshell, this book is all about...

Earning a living...

Building a career...

And Leading a life... .

Acknowledgments

A number of people have contributed directly and indirectly towards the development of this book. I am grateful to all of them.

My sincere gratitude to Heinz Meloth and Jayant Krishna, two people whom I would prefer to call my teachers at work. Thanks to J.K. Kharbanda, for inviting me to work with him. Thanks to Anant Jauhari for his empathy and to Sushil Prakash for his guidance and direction.

I would like to thank several of my friends and fellow entrepreneurs whose respective careers have been so much a part of this learning process and many of whose stories have become part of this book. In particular I would like to thank Girish Batra, Aviral Sinha, R. Suresh Kumar, Balakrishna S.K., Vikrant Nath, Rupak Sen, Rohit Kataria and Nischal Arora.

My respects to Dr D.V. Patvardhan, Ajoy Maharaj and to all my teachers for showing the way.

Special thanks to my brother, Vineet, for being there, at all the times. Without his help this dream could have never become a reality. To my parents, relatives and friends, to all of you I owe the success of this humble effort.

And finally, all this work would have gone in vain had not my publisher, Rupa & Co, taken so much interest in this project.

SECTION I

GETTING READY PHASE

1

Understanding the Basics

'The highest education is that which does not merely give us information but bring our life to harmony with all existence.'

Rabindra Nath Tagore

In this chapter we discuss the following:
1. What's Entrepreneurship?
2. How's Entrepreneurship different?
3. Can Entrepreneurship be nurtured?
4. Strength entrepreneurs possess

What's Entrepreneurship?

The dictionary says, *'Establishing and running a commercial venture to create wealth.'*

This seems to be a really simple and precise definition. However, the question is that if entrepreneurship can be explained and understood in such words, then why successful entrepreneurship is so scarce? If it is something so simple then why do so many, nearly as many as 70 per cent, entrepreneurial ventures fail within five years of their inception?

I feel entrepreneurial ventures fail in such great numbers because we have failed to understand entrepreneurship in its true sense and spirit. It is really unfortunate that traditionally entrepreneurship has always been talked of in reference to commercial ventures and as a distant synonym of self-employment. But this happens to be just one aspect of the subject.

The word 'entrepreneur' and subsequently 'entrepreneurship' has been derived from the word 'enterprise', which can be defined in five different ways.

a. An aggressive readiness to undertake taxing efforts
b. The wish, power and ability to begin and follow through with a plan or risk
c. Something undertaken, especially something requiring extensive planning and work
d. An exciting often hazardous undertaking
e. A commercial organization

Similarly the term entrepreneurship has more meanings attached to it than just what gets understood through the dictionary definition. In reality, entrepreneurship refers to a way of life. It is about doing something different and innovative and this innovation could be in any walk of life. It might sound amazing to some but it's true, that every businessman is not an entrepreneur and every entrepreneur is not a businessman.

Perhaps, the only way to understand what entrepreneurship is, is to look at it through the widest perspective over which it is applicable and subsequently relate that understanding to what we need to use it for, i.e. business entrepreneurship or to be more precise 'start-up business entrepreneurship'. And that is what we are going to do here.

At the outset let's forget everything we know about commercial ventures and the concept of wealth-creation. For the moment, let's approach the subject as if we know nothing about it. Let's de-learn to learn. Let's begin the journey with this wonderful story from the great epic of *Mahabharata*.

The epic of *Mahabharata* has thousands of characters, one of whom was Eklavya. Eklavya was a tribal boy, who had a dream. His dream was to be an ace archer; one whom no one could vanquish; the best in the world. His flair for the craft had become evident from his early childhood. However, to transform this latent potential into substantive performance he needed to learn under the supervision of an expert instructor for a few years.

Interestingly, Eklavya had somehow always envisioned Guru Drona to be his teacher. At that time, Guru Drona had been teaching the princes of Hastinapur kingdom – Arjuna, his brothers and their cousins.

With dream in his eyes and desire in the heart, one day Eklavya went to Guru Drona's Ashram. There he requested Guru Drona to accept him as one of his pupils. Guru Drona, however expressed his inability to oblige. He was bound by the terms of his Agreement with the King of Hastinapur, which forbade him from accepting anyone but the royal princes of the kingdom as his students.

Eklavya was immensely disappointed. However, he didn't lose heart and remained determined to learn. So, what did he do next? He went back to the forest. There he cleared a small piece of land and built a life-size clay statue of Guru Drona and then accepting the statue to be his Guru, he started practising... all on his own.

Every morning after offering his prayers to the statue, he would set himself a target, decide the distance to the target and then start shooting. He would keep shooting relentlessly from dawn until dusk, one target after another, increasing the level of difficulty with every little success, while reviewing the strategy at every little failure.

He would repeat his exercises without any break or gap every day, day after day, month after month, year after year. Soon he would not stop even at the fall of the day and would continue his practice further into the night, mastering the art of hitting targets in the dark. Such was the power of his resolve that slowly all the knowledge and skills started flowing to him instinctively, as if Guru Drona himself was actually standing there and teaching him everything.

Driven by his inner motivation, Eklavya kept practising with complete devotion and absolute faith determined to achieve what he had wished for. With the passage of time his hard work and devotion started bearing fruits and he started emerging as an ace archer, as keen and as sharp as Arjuna, widely perceived to be the best in those times.

Eklavya was no less an entrepreneur than anyone of us, because entrepreneurship is about a dream! Every entrepreneur, like Eklavya, starts the journey with nothing but a dream. Incidentally, the dream in itself has no value unless an actual attempt is made to transform it into reality. The process of transformation of this dream into reality is entrepreneurship.

To put it simply, entrepreneurship is an individual's resolve to keep working quietly in obscurity and amidst uncertainty, at times with negligible resources at disposal, to make a dream come true... some day.

In 1984 Rajendra Singh, then in his late 20s, left a cushy government job in Jaipur to do something useful and interesting in rural India. A five hour long bus journey brought him and four of his like-minded friends to Kishori village of Alwar district in Rajasthan. Still not sure what exactly to do, this team of young enthusiasts, amidst suspicion, distrust and hostility from local folks, started a few health and education programs in the village. Six months later a 60-year-old illiterate man named Mamu Patel came to Singh and said, "We don't need any school or medicine. If you really want to do something for us, pick up a spade and start digging."

Singh immediately decided to follow the advice, as he could see the wisdom behind it. Unfortunately his colleagues couldn't and as a result their association broke. Next morning Singh picked up a spade and went to dig, while his friends took a bus and went back to Jaipur. For the next six months, Singh kept digging, as Mamu Patel had wanted. No one joined him, as there were no young men around. The lack of water and opportunities in the village had made all of them migrate and Mamu Patel was too old to dig.

From his interactions with elders, Singh remembered that around 100 years back there was a big grain market in Alwar. Which meant that the land there must have been good and fertile with lots of water for irrigation. But now there was hardly any water in the area. The government had declared it a 'dark zone'. Singh realized that the tragedy could be converted into an opportunity if there was water and so he kept digging.

After six months, when some young men returned to work in fields during the monsoon, Mamu Patel convinced them to work with Singh in return for food-grain as wage, which Singh arranged through a few other NGOs working in the area. In three years time, together they made a huge pond that was fifteen feet deep.

When rains came, the pond filled up, simultaneously recharging the water table of the area. Soon, the wells started filling with water. Mamu Patel called all his relatives from the neighbouring villages just to see the visual impact and there was no looking back thereafter.

It had taken Rajendra Singh three years to build the first pond. In the fourth year 9 new ponds were added: 36 in fifth; 90 in sixth; 210 in seventh and the movement has not stopped even now. Today there are more than 3500 active ponds or 'jodhas', as villagers call them spread over 750 villages all around the area.

In 1995, government records had to be changed and the area was declared a 'white zone' as now the water was in plenty. The migration stopped; the five rivers flowing through the district that had long gone dry started flowing again; employment got regenerated in the areas of agricultural produce, vegetable marketing, basket weaving and fruit produce.

Rajendra Singh, a Ramon Magsaysay Awardee in 2001, continues to head the NGO Tarun Bharat Sangh (TBS) with several colleagues and volunteers and hasn't stopped digging. TBS today helps people identify their water-harvesting needs and assist them with projects, but only when the entire village has committed itself and pledged to meet half the costs. Aside from ponds, TBS helps villagers repair dams and deepen wells and mobilize them to plant trees on the hillsides to prevent erosion and restore the watershed; all using local skills and traditional technology, besides running a number of social, health and educational programs.

Entrepreneurship is about learning; learning from experiences; learning from circumstances and from surroundings. Quite similar to Rajendra Singh, no entrepreneur knows all the answers at the time of setting out on the journey. Yet they move out armed with just one weapon, called FAITH. They hold their faith in their ability to learn, which in turn keeps them steering ahead.

In other words, entrepreneurship is largely a game about learning, imbibing and implementing to achieve tangible results. Entrepreneurship is an individual's quest to acquire the mindset that allows him/her to grow even amidst chaos.

Rippan Kapur. Does that name ring a bell in your brain? May be not! Unfortunately Rippan Kapur is no more with us. He passed away on April 10, 1994 at a young age of forty. However, the institution he had started way back in 1979 with a mere Rs.50 (About US $ 5 in 1979) in his kitty still exists and continues to grow, touching lives of countless number of people, mostly destitute children all across India. In case you are still guessing, we are talking about CRY – Child Relief & You.

CRY had started its operations with Rippan as its only full time worker and his mother's dinning table as its first office in Mumbai. Today CRY has branches in five cities in India. In those initial days Rippan himself would do all the work. Today CRY operates through a network of volunteers, in partnerships with other NGOs, in alliances with Corporate bodies, besides having a workforce of its own.

In those initial days when CRY lacked infrastructure, Rippan would search for creative and often offbeat solutions to generate awareness about his programs. CRY's first fund-raising event **'Buy a brick, Build a School'** in 1980 was aimed at sensitizing privileged school children towards the needs of their lesser-privileged counterparts. In one of the subsequent years, CRY had brought three clowns from London to stage a travelling fund-raising show called Circus Magic, entertaining children through workshops.

Today all kind of events, viz., quizzes, plays, concerts, competitions, camps, jamboree, etc., are all regular features of CRY's fund raising programs. CRY had launched its greeting cards division in early 80's with no staff or infrastructure; today the organization has a strategic tie-up with Archies Greetings & Gifts for the purpose.

On the delivery side, CRY's focus has been primarily on education, bringing children to schools, terminating child labour, establishing non-formal education centers, supporting balwadis and generating support for disabled and special children.

As per it's annual report 2000-2001, CRY had mobilized deposits worth Rs.22.75 crore (US $ 4.5 million) through donations, sale of products and other promotional activities both within and outside India. It reached out to 1.2 lakh children spread over nearly 3000 villages and 720 urban slums through its 283 different initiatives being run across the country.

Rippan Kapur had never wanted CRY to be another personality-oriented organization. Thus he had always remained in the background and let CRY grow by leaps and bounds. He had always wanted CRY to be known for the work it does and so has it been!

Entrepreneurship is about networking. It is about developing systems to accomplish tasks. It is about bringing together necessary resources – men, machine and money, to achieve the desired objectives. It is about moving beyond the individual and mapping the growth path to create an enterprise that would generate value for all.

In other words, entrepreneurship is about leading, networking and consolidating the available resources to make best of the given opportunity. It is an individual's capacity to bring together diverse resources and create something valuable. To put things in a nutshell...

- Entrepreneurship is an individual's resolve to keep working in obscurity and amidst uncertainty to see a dream come true... some day.
- Entrepreneurship is an individual's quest to acquire the right mindset and learn to grow even amidst chaos.
- Entrepreneurship is an individual's capability to bring together diverse resources and create something valuable.

And finally...

Some time back, I had gone to attend a lecture on entrepreneurship by a famous Indian Entrepreneur from the

Silicon Valley. While delivering the address, the speaker suddenly shot a question to the audience: "What's entrepreneurship?"

"Keep the show running no matter what may come!" was the instant reply from somewhere towards the back of the hall.

The initial years of any start-up are most challenging ones. Ask any small time entrepreneur and they would tell you the hell they had to go through in those initial years. Many would even go on to confess that had they known what it takes to be successful in this career, they would have never embarked on to the journey in the first place. Nevertheless, people still get drawn towards entrepreneurship and people do succeed, and...so can you!

How's Entrepreneurship Different?

Is entrepreneurship only about personal qualities like individual's resolve, resilience, faith, patience, mindset etc.? What's unique about learning, imbibing and implementing or for that matter leading, networking and consolidating? Don't we need all this stuff to succeed anywhere, no matter what our choice of job or career might be? So why such a hue and cry about entrepreneurship? What makes entrepreneurship different?

Why do experts say that entrepreneurship is not a profession for everybody? What makes entrepreneurship such a mystery? What is it about entrepreneurship that's different from other professions? How's entrepreneurship different, say, from a normal salaried job?

To answer these questions and to understand the difference, let's visualize two hypothetical, yet real-life scenarios, one of Mr X and another of Ms Y.

Mr X has just received a job-offer from a reputed company to join its marketing team, while Ms Y has chosen to set-up her own marketing agency. Let's see how the two, although doing the same type of job, i.e. marketing and selling products, go about their careers in the due course of time.

He joins a team

The moment Mr X joins the Company, he becomes part of an already established team.

He gets taught

Mr X, being a new member of the team is taken through an orientation program where he learns about the company, its business, its business philosophy, its vision, mission and objectives, the market scenario, the competition, the customers and the job he is expected to carry out being part of the team.

He gets tartgets

Mr X, upon completing his training, is assigned a territory and given a target, which he is expected to achieve within a given period of time.

She starts alone

Ms Y begins alone and is expected to develop her own team (if any) over a period of time.

She must learn

Ms Y, the founder of the business, begins with defining her objectives. She conducts preliminary research to assess the market potential, the overall market scenario, the demand pattern, competition and other related issues. Based on her findings and her estimates, she defines her business, designs her road map and identifies her target customers.

She sets targets

Ms Y, being owner of the business decides her own targets, based on her perceptions of the market and then sets out to accomplish those targets.

He works following the rules

Mr X, while working follows business practices and philosophies as set for the employees of the company.

He has a job profile

Mr X works within the bounds of his job profile as defined by the company management.

He could survive being Master of One

Mr X doesn't have to worry about cross-functional responsibilities like HR, finance, legal, commercial, IT, etc., which gets taken care of by his colleagues. All he is expected to do is to focus on his job and do it well.

She design rules to work

Ms Y decides the kind of business practices and philosophies she would like to follow, based on her personal values and beliefs.

She can't have one

Ms Y can't have a fixed job profile. Everything or for that matter anything associated with her business would fall under her domain and she must attend to it.

She has also to be a Jack of All Trades

Ms Y has to be personally involved in carrying out all cross-functional responsibilities, besides doing what she specializes in, i.e. marketing products and she must do everything well to keep surviving.

The difference between the two situations is obvious. But being the author, it is my responsibility to spell them out distinctly for everyone to understand.

Success in any initiative, be it anywhere, requires two things working in tandem.

1. Strategic Thinking
2. Focused Action

For example, in *Mahabharata*, when Arjuna loses his sense of purpose, he seeks help from his friend and guide Krishna. Whereupon Krishna, 'the strategic thinker', guides Arjuna into performing 'focused action' to achieve the objective at the battlefield of Kurukshetra.

This is not some kind of an obscure or isolated example. In fact, we operate in a manner very similar to the one described above whenever we are a part of any organized network or group. Let's see through some common real-life examples.

- An infant cannot arrange for any of her needs by herself. It is for the parents to arrange for the infant's needs. Every parent provides for their child's comfort and growth to the best of their wisdom and ability (Strategic Thinking), while the infant accepts whatever has been arranged for her by the parents (Focused Action).

- In school it is our teachers who decide what we should be studying at what stage of our education and further how the lesson would be delivered to us and how our performance would be assessed (Strategic Thinking). We as students simply accept the verdict and go through the drill in a disciplined manner (Focused Action).

- Similarly when in a job, there are people at the top, who set the targets (Strategic Thinking), while we the ones below work to achieve those targets (Focused Action).

In all the three examples, the two things, 'Strategic Thinking' and 'Focused Action', get performed in tandem, however by different sets of people, like Krishna and Arjuna at the battlefield of Kurukshetra. Now compare this 'Krishna-Arjun' scenario with that of...

1. Lord Rama in his mission to conquer the mighty Ravana.
2. Mahatma Gandhi, while leading his fellow-countrymen in their freedom struggle against the British.
3. Mother Teresa, who dedicated her whole life for the cause of the poorest of the poor and went on to build an institution like 'Missionaries of Charity'.
4. Eklavya during his quest to become an ace archer.
5. Rajendra Singh working in obscurity to restore the degraded habitat of Alwar.
6. Rippan Kapur finding creative solutions to make a difference in the lives of thousands of destitute children.

Each of these people has not only been the chief 'Strategic Thinker' behind what they have been doing, but have also contributed to the mission by performing 'Focused Action'. *Business Entrepreneurs' fall in this category.* They are the people capable of performing the two things 'Strategic Thinking' and 'Focused Action' in tandem on their own.

Going back to our example of Mr X and Ms Y, we see that most of Mr X's concerns revolve around his working domain. He has a territory, a target and support of a team. He must work in his territory as per the guidelines laid down for him to achieve his target taking whatever help possible from his teammates (Focused Action). Whereas all the strategic thinking decisions concerning his work, issues like which business should the company run, which products should it sell, at what price, what should be the working practices within the company, etc., are decided by people placed higher up. In case Mr X wants to influence any of the strategic thinking decisions of the company, all he could do is – pass-on his suggestions to the decision-makers sitting at the top.

In contrast, Ms Y has to be worried about everything regarding her business. She does not only have to plan the business but execute the plan as well. In other words she must perform the two things 'Strategic Thinking' as well as 'Focused Action' in tandem all on her own to be successful.

It is this little complexity, of making the two things work in tandem on our own, that prevents entrepreneurship from being everybody's cup of tea.

Making the two things work in tandem on our own, might seem a child's play here on paper, but in real life it's not so. In case you don't believe me, self-assess your own life and the way you have been living. Look at the people around you. Most of them, you would find, prosper in some kind of an organised set up, being part of an established team.

In fact that's not something unusual. Most of us feel comfortable performing one thing at a time, while receiving support for the others from outside. No matter what we may say otherwise, we prefer to work in a 'Krishna-Arjuna' kind of team set-up. Very few people have the natural capability to build something valuable out of absolutely nothing. Those who can are fit to be labeled 'born entrepreneurs'.

Can Entrepreneurship Be Nurtured?

At the outset, what do we mean when we raise this question— Can entrepreneurship be nurtured? We simply mean—Can we learn to make the two things 'Strategic Thinking' and 'Focused Action' work in tandem on our own?

The answer is yes!

And that is what this book – *Accidental Entrepreneur* – is all about, helping people learn to make the two things 'Strategic Thinking' and 'Focused Action' work in tandem on their own and evolve as a successful entrepreneur.

If we study the lives and works of some of the most successful entrepreneurs, we would find that not all of them were born with the ability to make the two qualities work together in tandem. Instead most of them learned to do it, while still on the move and often at a heavy cost.

You don't believe me... go and ask... Henry Ford... if you can still find him around! Henry Ford could be labeled anything but definitely not a born entrepreneur. In fact I am yet to come across another person who goofed more number of times than this man did in his career. Yet the world remembers him as one of the most successful entrepreneurs of all times!*

Thus I am of the opinion that anyone can have a fair chance of succeeding as an entrepreneur, provided he/she is willing to learn the art of maintaining the right balance.

---

* We discuss the Henry Ford story later in Chapter 11.

Just in case you might have forgotten, entrepreneurship is the game of making something out of absolutely nothing. It is not a 100 meter dash, instead is a never-ending marathon, where the only way to win is to keep running. So let's shed all our fears of failure and move ahead with complete faith and the victory definitely shall be ours.

Strengths Entrepreneur Possess

Despite varying styles of working, successful entrepreneurs in the past have shown to possess certain common strengths. These are:

1. They are positive in their approach.
2. They are always open to new possibilities.
3. They create systems to accomplish tasks.
4. They possess high levels of energy and get sick far less than normal.
5. They are responsible people.
6. They acknowledge that they control their own destiny.
7. They have an understanding of what they do well and what they don't do well.
8. They would be willing to keep going when most people would rather give up.
9. They are never afraid to accept their mistakes.
10. They are quick learners.

We shall talk about entrepreneurial weaknesses in Chapter 6 – Blocking the Loopholes. For the time being I let you decide how you are going to use this information to the best of your advantage.

Five Points to Remember

Let's list the important points we have discussed in this chapter.

1. Besides establishing and running a commercial venture to create wealth, business entrepreneurship is:

    a. An individual's resolve to keep working in obscurity and amidst uncertainty to see a dream come true... some day.

    b. An individual's quest to acquire the right mindset and learn to grow even amidst chaos.

    c. An individual's capability to bring together diverse resources and create something valuable.

2. Success in any initiative, be it anywhere, requires two things working in tandem – 'Strategic Thinking' and 'Focused Action'. Under an organisational set-up the two functions get performed by two different sets of people, like Krishna and Arjuna at the battlefield of Kurukshetra. However entrepreneurs, like Lord Rama, must know to perform the two functions in tandem by themselves. It is this little complexity which makes entrepreneurship a specialized profession.

3. Not all of us are born with the ability to make the two things – 'Strategic Thinking' and 'Focused Action' work in tandem on our own. However we can always learn the same and can evolve as a successful entrepreneur.

4. Entrepreneurship can be nurtured and anyone can have a fair chance of succeeding in the profession, provided he/she is willing to learn the art of maintaining the right balance.

5. Finally, as already stated, entrepreneurship is not a 100 meter dash; instead it is like a never-ending marathon.

This brings us to the end of this chapter. In our next chapter we discuss 'How to choose the business best suited for us?'

2

The Best Business to Start

'The people who get on in this world are the people who get up and look for the circumstances they want, and, if they can't find them, make them.'
George Bernard Shaw

In this chapter we discuss the following:
1. Which business is the best business?
2. Six Steps to choose the right business.
3. How NOT to choose a business.
4. Making the right choice – An Anecdote.
5. The case of Accidental Entrepreneurs.

Which Business is the Best Business?

Take my word for it, as a first-generation entrepreneur, one thing you would never fall short of would be free-of-cost and unasked-for advice on 'Which business should you be starting.'

You would always keep receiving suggestions like...
- Why don't you open a Cyber Café?
- Cyber-Café is a thing of past... start a Call-Centre!
- Get into IT... that's the IN-thing?
- Don't enter IT... its DEAD!
- Why don't you take franchise of some big "multi-national" company?
- Saw that ad in the Newspaper, they are looking for marketing partners... Why don't you apply?
- Why don't you start the same business, the one that Mr Mathur's son is doing?
- Kumar has made so much money in that business... Why don't you start something like that?

Interestingly, most of these suggestions would come from people who have either no or simply some peripheral entrepreneurial experience. Unfortunately that's not all! Once you have chosen a line of business, be it anything, the same people would be back again at your doorsteps, presenting their uncalled-for critical appraisal on your choice.
- What kind of business is that?
- Do you know anyone else doing it?
- Does it have any scope over here?
- Who buys that? How many people would need it?
- There's so much competition in this field... you won't be able to survive!
- This won't work? You have chosen a wrong business?
- Why don't you start something in parallel, besides whatever you are doing?... And so on.

Rule 1: Get rid of all such uninvited advisors with immediate effect

Mind you, it might not be an easy thing to do, but it must be done. Many of your advisors might be people of great social and professional prominence, none of whom you could afford to offend. So you must learn to deal with them very tactfully. Listen carefully to everybody; weigh the merits/demerits of every suggestion under the given set of circumstances; however don't get carried away by any suggestion that might come your way. Use your way. Use your WISDOM before taking a decision.

Some of your advisors might be genuine well wishers. Such people would always honestly tell what they think is good for you. But then even in these cases, what counts in the end is what YOU actually believe in and would want to do.

Unemployment is a highly depressing situation. Prolonged unemployment could make any person feel helpless, weak and unwanted from inside. It is not always easy for people running low on self-confidence and self-esteem to take such a firm stand. Instead it is natural for people in this state of mind to get swayed by soft promotions, especially the ones that show the grass to be greener on the other side of the fence. But then the grass has always looked greener on the other side of the fence, so there are no prizes for getting carried away!

There are primarily three kinds of people in this world:
1. Those who make things happen.
2. Those who watch things happen.
3. Those who wonder what happened.

If you have chosen to be an entrepreneur then you must belong to the first category and start making things happen. Take charge of your destiny, use your wisdom, feel responsible and start making things happen.

Coming back to our question: *Which business is the best business?*

The answer is **One that you feel suits you the best!**

Please remember that there are no good businesses or bad businesses, no hot businesses or cold businesses, no hep businesses or dud businesses; instead just good decisions and bad decisions.

The question at this stage is—what makes for a 'good decision' or a 'bad decision' when choosing a business? This is what we shall keep discussing in detail throughout this and also the next chapter. However, for the time being...

Any decision on the choice of business must be taken only after rounds of rational thinking and pragmatic analysis. You could ask others for their opinion. However, never get carried away by what they might say. In the end always let your own judgment prevail over everything else. Never take things for granted, always question what might look obvious. Don't rush to any conclusions, take your own time and get set to take charge of your destiny.

Any business could be a successful business, provided you as an entrepreneur believe in it passionately.

Throughout this book we shall keep discussing cases of several entrepreneurs, who got into what people would otherwise call unusual businesses. But they have been immensely successful in their ventures, primarily because they went out to do something, which they had always passionately believed in and thus could lend their spirit to their work.

This brings us to the question—How to know which is the best business for us? How do we hunt/narrow down on to the business that might suit us the best? How to know what we might passionately believe in?

Let's try finding answers to the above questions.

While choosing a business the decision has to be made on two fronts:

1. The nature of the business – Manufacturing, Trading, Retailing, Marketing, Service provider, Consultancy, Outsourcing, etc.

2. The choice of the industry – Telecom, Insurance, Tourism, Courier, Packaging, Construction, Media, Hospitality, etc.

In many cases it is the choice of industry that decides the nature of business and vice-versa. For example, if you want to be an insurance agent you don't need to start a factory. Similarly, if you are a die-hard manufacturing freak, tourism or insurance won't be the industry for you. Nevertheless, no matter whatever the case may be, a decision has to be taken on both the fronts.

Six Steps to choose the best business

1. Define your Purpose.
2. Identify your Interests.
3. Study your Background.
4. Weigh your Resources.
5. List your Options.

6. Take a Decision.

Let's discuss each of the above in detail.

Step 1. Define your Purpose

Ask yourself *Why am I getting myself into self-employment?*

- Is it because I am unemployed and need a vocation to earn a living.
- Is it because I must remain busy with something till I find a suitable employment.
- Is it because I want to build a career pursuing a dream/ambition.
- Is it because that's the way I want to lead my life.
- Is it because I want to earn a lot of name, fame and money.
- Is it because I want to do something challenging/different.
- Is it because I have an idea, which I feel could be converted into a profitable business proposition.
- Is it because I have some money, which I would like to invest in a business.
- Is it a bit of all the above; or
- Is it none of the above at all.

Your purpose would play a big role in deciding your choice of the business. For example, if you are logging on to self-employment because you have been unemployed and need to have a work to earn a living, you are likely to be willing to start with anything small and simple and make it grow with time.

But if your reason for getting onto self-employment is to earn a lot of money very quickly, then you might only be satisfied with some kind of a really radical business idea, which promises potential for growth in exponential terms and that would make your choice of business more difficult.

Whatever be your answer to the above question, try defining your purpose as clearly as possible. Keep it compact, simple and accurate. It must be measurable, realistic and down-to-earth. The more clearly you define your purpose, easier it shall be for you to make a final decision.

Step 2: Identify your Interests

Instead of narrating a commentary, let me just quote a few examples to highlight the role your hobbies and interests could play in deciding your choice of business/profession.

- **Ram Gopal Verma,** the famous Indian movie director, after completing his B.Tech in civil engineering, opened a video library. He would spend all his time watching cassettes in his library, trying to learn the art of movie making. Disturbed by his behaviour, at one stage, his parents had seriously contemplated taking him to a psychiatrist. However his interest was in making films and that is what he eventually chose as his career.

- **Harsha Bhogle,** the famous cricket commentator, would deliver commentary at local cricket matches in his hometown Hyderabad. Sometimes he would record his own voice and drop the cassettes at the local radio station. Later, he worked for a company owned by Sunil Gavaskar, the legendary cricketer, for several years. However, during this period he got to meet Gavaskar only on two occasions. Today Harsha Bhogle is a leading TV commentator, who commentates regularly along with Gavaskar and other great cricketers. We see Bhogle in the commentary-box just because of his intense interest in that type of work.

- Those who have lived in Delhi would have most likely heard the famous radio jockey **Shamshir Rai Luthra** (of the 'Das Se Gyaraha' fame). Shamshir Rai Luthra besides being an anchor runs a media school and conducts workshops on effective communication and personality development. When in school he was labeled as the most talkative child in the class. Today he owes all his success to the very same quality, i.e. his ability to talk, for which he was regularly snubbed at school.

We have always been told to treat our work as worship. It is true that when work is done in the spirit of worship, the quality of work undergoes a metamorphosis. As a result, even ordinary work gets transformed from a mere chore to an extraordinary reality.

Unfortunately, the limitations of human nature restrict us from treating every work as worship. So let's choose the work that we can actually treat as worship and enjoy its fruits. Such a work could only be something in which we feel deeply interested. So watch-out for your interests! The history of entrepreneurship is full of people who have converted their hobbies and interests into successful professions/businesses. You could well be the next.

Step 3: Study your Background

- **Dr John Smith Pemberton** chose to sell a sweet carbonated liquid called Coca-Cola because he was a pharmacist and had spent half his life inventing this wonder drink.

- **Karl Benz** chose to manufacture and sell automobiles because he was an engineer and had spent half his life inventing, designing and driving automobiles.
- **M.S. Oberoi**, the founder of the Oberoi Group of Hotels, got into the hospitality business because he had started his career as an employee of a small hotel and had spent a great amount of time understanding the needs of that particular industry.
- **Prannoy Roy** formed NDTV and started making News Magazines because he had been a journalist all his life and thus could visualize a business opportunity in the same field.

When we talk about background then it not only includes the educational or professional background, but also the social as well as the family background. Assess your strengths and weaknesses. Identify what you can do well and what you cannot. Every business is not for everybody, but there would always be a business, which is for you.

Example:

Do you remember the Coca-Cola commercial a few years back featuring Hrithik Roshan, the movie star, juggling with the coke bottles! Do you know who taught him the juggler's tricks! Well, a student of Shathbi Basu. Naturally the question you would ask is who's **Shathbi Basu?**

Shathbi Basu, a graduate in hotel management had a passion for bartending. Unfortunately, not any of the good hotels even in a cosmopolitan Mumbai were willing to take the risk of introducing a lady bartender till even a few years back. This was despite an acute shortage of adequate professional talent in the field.

Sensing the opportunity, the lady set up an institute for teaching people how to be an expert bartender. Shathbi Basu owns and runs the **STIR Academy of Bartendering** in Mumbai. Her students come from all over the country and abroad. In fact, many of her students themselves are now experts in their own way, like the one who taught a few tricks to Hrithik Roshan for the Coca-Cola commercial. Today the lady is credited with making bartending a serious and attractive profession in India and yes, now there are many women working as successful bartenders across the country.

Step 4: Weigh your Resources

An unemployed teacher, divorced, living on public assistance in a tiny flat in Edinburgh with her infant daughter, started writing at a table in a café, while her daughter was taking a nap. Thanks to the paltry grant from the Scottish Arts Council, she could somehow manage to continue her work beyond the coffee table and turn it into a book. It took J.K. Rowling five years to complete *Harry Potter and the Sorcerer's Stone...* The rest is history.

J.K. Rowling has been recognized for her literary contributions all over the world. Here we pay our tribute to the lady for her contributions to the field of self-employment. Numerous entrepreneurs in the past have made their journey from rags to the riches. Have you wondered what has been the secret of their success?

These people succeed because they have always remembered a word from the English dictionary, it's called 'Feasible' and means 'practicable, possible'. At the same time they never forgot the little statement we mentioned at the beginning of this chapter by G.B. Shaw which says, 'The people who get on in this world are the people who get up and look for the circumstances they want, and, if they can't find them, make them.'

There surely is a catch... So catch it quick!

There are professional activities, which can be started with no monetary investments, like the one J.K. Rowling chose (writing). On the other hand there are business activities, which require huge amounts of monetary investment and deployment of diverse resources, like the ones chosen by Henry Ford or even Ram Gopal Verma. Your choice of business must be in harmony with the resources you have at your disposal. Otherwise first get the resources and only then start.

One of the most wonderful examples of generating necessary resources before starting a business could be observed from the life and collective success of two gentlemen, whose first names were Henry and Charles.

Henry, who had started working at an age of nine, selling newspapers, went on to run a successful electrical and mechanical business. He had a passion for technology and somehow developed a fancy for automobiles. Unfortunately he didn't have any technical knowledge about automobiles. In order to learn more about automobile engines, he bought himself a second hand car and started by dismantling it completely. A few years later, on the April fool's day, 1904, he test-drove his first self-designed creation.

All this time Charles, who had also been a gold-medallist auto-racer, had been busy selling quality cars to rich people completely unaware of Henry and his latest invention. He was an expert salesman, who had become fully aware of the tastes of the rich and famous. Henry needed someone who could help him sell his new creation, while Charles needed a product that could make him stand out in the ever-growing crowd of auto-sellers. Both of them had acquired necessary resources in two related aspects of the same business.

As they say, nothing can stop the idea whose time has come! A series of strange coincidences brought the two of them together and on December 23, 1904 they signed an agreement and soon The Silver Ghost was on the roads. Well, that's the story of **Henry Rolls** and **Charles Royce**.

Step 5: List your Options

Once you have analyzed your interests, studied your background and weighed your resources, list all your options along with their positives and negatives. You might have quiet a few, so now its time to narrow down on to one. How do we do that? We evaluate the odds against each.

Ask Yourself:

Does this business have a growing market? For example, selling 'typewriters' might not prove to be a healthy business in the present times, however selling mobile phones, computers or laptops might just be.

Is the market good enough to allow viable operations? For example, you would definitely bomb selling air-conditioners in rural/semi-urban areas but might just do great selling tractors or agricultural equipment in the same market.

Would the returns match my expectations? A very difficult question to answer. Nevertheless, it's always better to have rational and realistic expectations, pragmatic enough to be realized.

Step 6: Take a Decision

At the time of making the final decision, ask yourself:

1. Do I passionately believe in this line of business?
2. Can I generate a distinct competitive advantage to survive in the market?
3. Can I confidently manage it on my own?

If the answer to all the three questions is YES, then move ahead... otherwise look for other options.

How NOT to select a business?

Never choose a business just because it's on a hype

Never choose a business just because someone else has been successful in it

Never choose a business just because it promises quick and/or huge returns

The story of the dot.com age:

The greatest hype of the recent times was the dot.com boom. It was a hype at the global scale. The period of six years (1996-2001) witnessed a sudden surge in the entrepreneurial activity all across the globe. Inspired by the over-night success of a few blue eyed boys, hoards of people rushed to grab a slice of the cake. Everything that was worth anything was dot.commed without a miss. However where are those dot.com boys today! How many people eventually joined the league of Sabeer Bhatia and Jeff Bezos? Perhaps only a handful. Those who could survive were mostly the people who had got their fundamentals correct from the very beginning.

Unfortunately we human beings have a strong tendency to follow what is called the 'herd mentality'. The moment anything is a success anywhere, everyone wants to imitate it immediately. For instance, soon after the dot.com bubble had burst, we saw a sudden thrust towards what has since been named ITES (IT Enabled Services), which include ventures like Call Centres, Business Process Outsourcing outfits, etc. This industry grew 71 per cent in India in 2001-02 with a total turnover of about Rs.7500 crore ($ 1.5 billion), a year in which the traditional software industry grew by only 18 per cent. And suddenly everyone wanted to be on-board, from blue-chip corporates to over enthusiastic entrepreneurs, everyone announced their plans to join the ITES bandwagon.

Today, even less than two years down the road, we are facing a serious problem of excessive capacity in this sector, where the returns are not likely to match the investments being made. The things are reaching such a stage that our over-opportunism about the sector is threatening to erode the country's competitiveness in the business.

The moral of the story:
No matter how exciting the opportunity might appear from the outside, never enter unless you are considerably sure of what you are getting yourself into.

Any opportunity could be a hot opportunity provided you have understood the needs of the business in totality.

Making the Right Choice – An Anecdote

Here I would like to narrate the case of two fellow entrepreneurs, Suresh Kumar and Dileep Kumar of Imtech Industries, Trivandrum. Suresh, a graduate engineer, had spent nearly seven years working for an electronic bookbinding-machine manufacturing company, first at the shop-floor level and then in the marketing department. A proficient engineer and a keen marketer, he not only helped his employer company sell a large number of machines all over the country but in the process also built a good rapport in the market. A petty disagreement with the management made him quit his job in 1998-99. The job was lost and the entrepreneur was born. All this time Dileep, a qualified finance professional had been working in the finance department of the same company.

Identifying a long-existing gap in the demand pattern, they decided to come out with a 100 per cent electro-mechanical machine (no electronic components) that was capable of competitive performance, but would cost far less than an electronic-version machine. They targeted this new product towards small and medium sized presses and bookbinders. Their initial plan was to keep selling one machine per month for the first two years. Today, three years later, they have sold over fifty machines across the country and a few abroad as well. In the process their original product has improved several folds and now they have started competing neck-to-neck with global giants in the field like Kolbus, Hedilburg and Wellbound.

Today when we look back we can see four distinct things that helped Suresh and Dileep succeed:

1. They ventured into a business about which they knew everything.
2. They identified a gap, where they could generate a distinct competitive advantage.
3. As a result they could design a product that their customers were already waiting for.
4. In the end they did something, which they had always believed in and had always wanted to do.

The Case of Accidental Entrepreneurs

In the above example it was easy for Suresh and Dileep to take a decision primarily because they had been working in that particular industry for a good number of years. As a result they knew the market inside-out and understood its demands. Their experience helped them design a product that was readily acceptable to the prospective customers.

However, when we talk in reference to accidental entrepreneurs, there could be a sizable number of people who might not have any prior work-experience or any special professional qualification to bank upon. Further, there might be people with no specific area of specialization or even a particular interest or hobby that could be converted immediately into a profession. What business could such people start?

At the outset, the situation might look grim, but in reality the number of options even for this category of people are unlimited. Taking an appropriate decision might prove to be a painful and lengthy process, but then making a decision on what business to choose is seldom a spontaneous one for anybody. Most people take some time to decide and many, including yours truly, often learn only the hard way, i.e. after making a couple of costly mistakes.

Here are 5 simple tips which can help accidental entrepreneurs take a right decision at the right time, matching their skills and resources. This is besides the six steps we discussed earlier in the chapter.

1. Choose a business which could be started small.
2. Choose a business which would need minimum monetary investment.
3. Choose a business which is simple to run.
4. Choose a business which could be gradually grown.
5. Choose a business which is easy to quit.

The idea should be to start with something small, learn on-the-job, and grow gradually. Don't get blindly attracted by some business idea that promises quick or very huge returns. Please remember that there are no free lunches on offer anywhere. Your first aim should be to learn and gain some hands-on experience of running the real thing. Once you have got your basics in place, you won't have any difficulty scaling up the operations at any stage.

The final message:

If you lack depth in your experience then devote some time to your training and learning, before making the final choice!

For the rest, we talk in detail about entrepreneurial education in the next chapter – The Best Time to Start.

Five Points to Remember

To sum up what we have discussed in this chapter:

1. Which business is the best business? The answer is *'One that you feel suits you the best!'* Any business could be a successful business, provided you as an entrepreneur believe in it passionately.

2. An entrepreneur must essentially follow six steps in choosing a business. These are–
   a. Define your Purpose
   b. Identify your Interests
   c. Study your Background
   d. Weigh your Resources
   e. List your Options
   f. Take a Decision.

3. At the time of making the final decision, ask yourself:
   a. Do I passionately believe in this line of business?
   b. Can I generate a distinct competitive advantage to survive in the market?
   c. Can I confidently manage it on my own?

4. Never enter a business unless you are considerably sure of what you are getting yourself into. Any opportunity could be a hot opportunity provided you have understood the needs of the business in totality.

5. If you lack depth in your experience then devote some time to your training and learning, before making the final choice. Your plan should be to start with something small, learn on-the-job, and grow gradually over a period of time.

   This brings us to the end of this chapter. In our next chapter we talk about how to decide the right time to start the business.

3

The Best Time to Start

'We say Newton discovered gravitation. Was it sitting anywhere in a corner waiting for him? It was in his own mind; the time came and he found out.'
Swami Vivekanand

In this chapter we discuss the following:
1. What's the best time to start?
2. Two misconceptions
3. The Eternal Dilemma
4. Why necessarily allow some preparation time?
5. Work Experience – How important could it be?
6. Can jobless people gain work experience?

What's The Best Time to Start?

What's the best time to start? This question reminds me the case of a close friend. This friend had always wanted to be a businessman. As soon as he finished his studies, he started searching for an appropriate business.

After some preliminary research and informal consultations he decided to begin with a small retail outlet. His idea was to gain some hands-on experience of running an actual business and then subsequently move on to some kind of a bigger, viz., wholesale/franchise/manufacturing business. Keeping in line with this master plan, the family made a quick investment in purchasing a 100 sq.ft. retail space in a neighbourhood shopping complex.

Interestingly, we the people in India have this habit of consulting our astrologers before commencing anything important and in this case our friend was no exception. So in came the family astrologer, who advised my friend to start his business before a certain date, which was incidentally coming within two weeks; failing which, the astrologer had told that he would not be able to start anything for the next several years.

My friend, a noble fellow, had never been afraid of challenges. He took his astrologer's advice in the same spirit and did actually manage to lift the curtains on the auspicious date. Unfortunately, not much went well after that auspicious day. Three years down the road, my friend finally closed down the business and took to a different career. The question is... what went wrong!

I feel everything from the start. Firstly he had hardly prepared himself for the job. He had hardly spent any time studying the market, understanding his customers and planning the business. Lack of absolute knowledge made him start with only an optimistic picture in his mind rather than a realistic one. As a result there was a big mismatch between what he had originally expected and what he actually got out of the venture. This in turn created disillusionment and it was not long before that his interest in the business started fading and he began looking for an alternate career.

The moral of the story:
Do not begin unless you have made yourself fully aware of all the needs and requirements of the up-coming business.

Any moment could be the auspicious moment, provided you have done your homework well in advance.

Two Misconceptions

At this stage it would be interesting to talk about two misconceptions, which tempt entrepreneurs to kick-off their ventures before they actually should.

Misconception No. 1: *Entrepreneurs are big risk takers.*

Contrary to the widespread belief, successful entrepreneurs are not big risk takers; instead they are expert risk hedgers. Risk is something, which is inevitable to any entrepreneurial venture, thanks to the uncontrollable external environment. Expert entrepreneurs know this fact and thus avoid adding anything to an already volatile system at least from their side; instead they work to reduce the overall uncertainty by regulating the controllable parameters of the internal environment.

Successful entrepreneurs investigate their SWOT (Strength, Weaknesses, Opportunities and Threats) in clear and tangible terms. They use their strengths to offset as many weaknesses and make sure that the opportunities always outnumber the threats. They invest in building capability and keep creating new openings to stay in business.

Hedging in an entrepreneurial environment is more of an art, than a science. All it requires is some practice, some perseverance and a lot of common sense. We shall discuss more about various hedging techniques in the subsequent chapters.

Misconception No. 2: *Opportunity doesn't strike twice.*

I am not questioning the axiom, instead the question I want to raise here is—How ready are you to make best of the opportunity, when it strikes? Because if you're not 100 per cent prepared, then any opportunity is as good as 'No Opportunity'! Thus in order to make best of any opportunity we must first acquire the skills and gather the resources needed for the job, before actually jumping on to the bandwagon.

Opportunities would always be there in one form or the other, however unless we have carefully prepared ourselves for the mission there is no way we could utilize them to our benefit. Please remember that it is not enough to come to the river intending to fish, you have to bring a net also.

The Eternal Dilemma

I have an uncle (father's friend). He has been working with a well-known corporate house for over 30 years now and has performed extremely well in his job. He enjoys enormous reputation within and outside the company. Interestingly, ever since I was a child, I remember him talking about starting his own business... some day. I remember those long discussions across the coffee table, discussing various possibilities, evaluating new ideas and assessing viability. My uncle possessed all the attributes needed to be an entrepreneur; yet he could never start a business. I had always wondered, why?

Unable to figure out the answer on my own, I decided to take the question to him. So one day, judging him to be in a good mood, I put across this question directly to him, "Why couldn't you start?"

He gave my question some thought and said, "I could never do away with the security of a well-paid job. I could never prepare myself to embrace a little uncertainty. I could never get over the fear of failure. I could never generate enough faith to follow my conviction and now it's most unlikely that I would ever be able to. Perhaps, I have waited far too long!"

This brings us to the eternal dilemma budding entrepreneurs' face. If they start too quickly, they might end up burning their fingers! If they wait too long, they might never be able to start! So what is the ideal preparation time one should allow for striking the right balance.

Every entrepreneur must allow a time of at least five to six months, after conceiving the business idea and before actually kicking-off the venture.

Getting excited upon hitting a new idea is a natural human propensity, especially when the idea promises to extol some hidden potential. Often people get carried away under the influence of excitement and fail to look at the flip side of the idea. A period of five to six months is ideal because if you can keep an idea alive in your mind for so long and still feel enthusiastic about it, it is most likely that you have hit the right idea.

Some business concepts, especially the ones that require heavy deployment of resources might demand for a much longer preparation time. However, in such cases a decision would have to be taken by the individual entrepreneur based on their wisdom and their level of comfort.

All the same, don't keep waiting for things to get too comfortable, otherwise even you might end up just like my uncle.

At this stage a question might arise in the minds of some readers: Why Necessarily Allow Some Time for Preparation?

In a job scenario, all good organizations, prescribe a period of probation for its new entrants, especially for those starting their first job. The companies use this period to impart training to their new recruits and to familiarize them with the working practices and philosophies of the organization. This period is also used to assess the preliminary potential of every individual employee.

The first generation entrepreneurs should see this preparatory period as their probation to entrepreneurship and utilize the time to investigate deeply about their prospective business idea. This period should be used to gather valuable information about the product, customers, market, suppliers and the industry as a whole. It should be used to study and understand the processes that would be involved in running the business. For example, things like, comprehending the business cycle, studying the channels for the flow of goods and money, identifying the established business practices of the industry/market, etc.

Secondly, this time should be used to harness personal skills, knowledge and abilities in congruence with the needs of your upcoming business. For example, if you don't know how to keep the books of account, which you would be required to do while running your venture, then utilize this time to learn the same.

Thirdly, this time should be utilized to identify the potential loopholes or the possible glitches in the business idea. The question might be—How do we do that? The answer is—By utilizing the positive power of negative thinking.

Just ask yourself, "What would I do if I fail?"

This should lead you to ask yourself, "Under what circumstances could I possibly fail?"

And further, "How could I avoid getting into any of these circumstances?"

... and so on.

Lastly, logging on to self-employment means bringing a big change in your life. You might have to invest money from your personal savings or pledge/mortgage personal assets to secure funds for operations. Further, your business would take time to start producing regular returns.

As an entrepreneur it's your duty to safeguard yourself and your family against these financial uncertainties. Unfortunately, we don't have any well-set social security structure in our country, which could allow for any cover. Thus every entrepreneur must utilize this time to assess his/her requirements in terms of social or family obligations and make arrangements for the same. Allow yourself some cushion in terms of financial savings (if possible) before you venture out on your own.

Work Experience – How Important Could It Be?

In the previous chapter, while discussing the case of accidental entrepreneurs we had mentioned briefly about the virtues of prior work experience. Here we take up the subject in its complete detail. Prior work experience of a few years (at least four to six) could help entrepreneurs on four accounts.

- Firstly, there are things that can be learnt only by being in a situation and not from any book or in the classroom. These are the various ground-level real-life practical complexities associated with the day-to-day running of business. Being in a job for a few years can bring entrepreneurs face to face with these realities of getting things done in practical terms.

- Secondly, an entrepreneur has not only to be a 'Master of One', but simultaneously also a 'Jack of All'. By the virtue of working in an established organization one gets the opportunity to observe the other organizational functions and responsibilities, different from the area of one's specialization. For example, even if you might be in the marketing department, you would have to interact with Finance, HR or Legal departments to get your things done. These interactions could give you valuable insight into the cross-functional requirements of running any business, which you would be required to perform at the time of running your own venture.

- Thirdly, most entrepreneurial ventures fail because the entrepreneurs promoting the venture lose faith in prospects of the business. They get disillusioned mid-way and start losing interest. Normally such things happen when an entrepreneur fails to map his/her expectations from the venture correctly. Some years of working in the field can help people learn to draw realistic estimates and thus not lead to disillusionment at a later stage.

- Lastly, the long-term survival of any entrepreneurial venture depends on the harmony the entrepreneur is able to derive between the internal and the external business environment. The external environment is uncontrollable and cannot be influenced. Thus adjustments are to be made on the internal front. This is purely an art of management, which can only be understood by being part of the ever-changing business environment. Hence a work experience of a few years could be highly useful for the purpose.

The best thing about being in somebody's employment is that while you learn your employer bears the cost of your learning. In contrast, when self-employed you learn as well as bear the cost of your own learning.

I recall the case of a colleague from my tenure with an Export House. This colleague, Neeraj Sharma, was working in the garments division of the company as a merchandiser. He was highly proficient at his work and was quite a sought after man in his department. The interesting thing about Neeraj was his habit of bombarding people with his inquisitive questions. Not only would he ask others questions about their work, but would also offer his services, in case they ever needed his help. In a small company, where managing crisis was a routine job, it had proved to be a really generous offer. His constant interaction with the people of other departments soon made him highly aware of various practical aspects of running a business.

Initially I would not understand the reason behind his strange behaviour, but now I do. Today Neeraj is a proud owner of a small ready-made garment manufacturing unit, which he runs in partnership with his sister, who is a fashion designer. As per his own admission, the experience gained out of those limited but highly focused interactions with his colleagues in accounts, finance, marketing and HR departments have helped him manage his business more effectively.

The above example seems good for the people who can manage some kind of employment. But our book is about accidental entrepreneurs, i.e. the people who wish to take to entrepreneurship because of unemployment. So we must also talk about the worst case scenario. Can unemployed people gain work-experience?

Can Jobless People Gain Work Experience?

Why not! Simply volunteer to work!

Two months into my tenure of unemployment, I discovered to my horror that I was getting out of touch with the things happening around. I realized that I had become a mere bystander, watching the action from outside and not being part of it in the middle of the ring. It was a terrible 'sinking' feeling, for suddenly I had been reduced to a Nobody!

I needed to find a way out of the muddle immediately. Luckily, the very next morning I banged into my neighbour at the milk booth. After exchanging the normal pleasantries, my neighbour, a teacher by profession, asked me if I knew someone who could help him organize a children's fair being scheduled by his School. He was looking for someone who could work as a part-time Coordinator of the event. It was an opportunity and without bothering to know any more details, I volunteered instantaneously and the offer was accepted immediately with pleasure.

For the next four weeks I worked with the school, doing all kinds of coordination and PR work in return for a sumptuous afternoon lunch, unlimited number of tea/coffee and a stipend of Rs.100 per day (US $ 2.10).

Honestly speaking, I have never in my career ever felt so happy and satisfied as I had during those four weeks. I felt happy because I was once again back in the ring. I was proving useful to others and they seemed happy to have my services. There were things happening all around and I was in middle of it all. I was learning, doing and achieving, all at the same time. No more did I remain a – Nobody. Instead I had learned the secret of being at least – Somebody.

Thereafter I worked with several other agencies doing different kind of jobs, many times for no monetary returns at all. Today I find these assignments to be some of the most valuable experiences of my professional life. The lessons learnt at these places have proved to be a significant milestone in shaping my subsequent career.

Now I am a self-employed professional earning a decent living, but still I do volunteer for certain activities at diverse platforms. I set some time out of my schedule to be part of these monetarily non-remunarative activities, where I simply volunteer to work. For instance, I am an active member of a management association, editor of a newsletter and webmaster of a website.

People often ask me, why do I do this! I tell them, just for the heck of it! But in reality, my voluntary associations have taken me to people and places, with whom otherwise I could have in no way come face-to-face. This has helped me immensely in my business as well. Please remember;

word-of-mouth publicity is still the most powerful advertising tool. An added advantage is that it doesn't cost a penny. Genuine good work done in a positive spirit gets appreciated more that you could even imagine now!

So what are you waiting for, if you are busy doing nothing, get up and look around. There would definitely be somebody who would be willing to take your services... if they come for free! Gain your experience and move ahead!

It might sound a bit harsh, but then, beggars can't be choosers! Hence it is important that you make best of every opportunity that you get. No matter how meek the opportunity might be, you can always make the best of it... only if you believe in it and go into it with a positive frame of mind.

This brings us to the end of this chapter. Let's summarize what we have been discussing here.

Five Points To Remember

1. Do not begin unless you have made yourself fully aware of all the needs and requirements of the up-coming business. Any moment could be the auspicious moment, provided you have done your homework well in advance.

2. Contrary to the widespread belief, successful entrepreneurs are not big risk takers; instead they are expert risk hedgers. Further, an entrepreneur must get equipped in advance before venturing to exploit an opportunity.

3. Every entrepreneur must allow a time of at least five to six months, after conceiving the business idea and before actually kicking-off the venture. This period should be used:

a. To gather valuable information about the product, customers, market, suppliers and the industry as a whole.

b. To harness personal skills, knowledge and abilities in congruence with the needs of your upcoming business.

c. To identify the potential loopholes or the possible glitches in the business idea.

d. To safeguard yourself and your family against the financial uncertainties that are likely to follow once you start the business.

4. Prior work experience of a few years could help entrepreneurs on several accounts at the time of running their business.

5. If you don't have proper work-experience, gain some by working at least for a few months. Volunteer to work for anything you get! Your objective should be to get a feel of the actual work environment and know the way things get done. Gain your experience and move ahead.

With this we close this chapter and incidentally also the 'Getting-Ready Phase'. Next chapter onwards we enter the 'Planning Phase', where we talk about planning related issues associated with a start-up business venture.

SECTION II

PLANNING PHASE

4

Evolving the Plan

'When men speak of the future, the Gods laugh!'
                                    A Chinese Proverb

In this chapter we discuss the following:
  1. What's planning?
  2. Why should I write my Business Plan?
  3. How big should be this written Business Plan?
  4. Designing the Business Plan.
  5. The first step – Identifying the Objectives.

What's Planning?

Let's once again go back into the times of *Mahabharata* and to the class of Guru Drona.

Guru Drona, who had been teaching archery to the princes of Hastinapur kingdom, one day, decided to call his students for a test. He hung a sparrow made of wood from the branch of a tree some distance away and told his students to hit the bird in its eye. The princes understood the task and accordingly lined-up to take their turn at the test.

First came Yudhistir, the eldest prince with his bow and arrow. He stood at the designated spot and took the aim, awaiting his Guru's instructions to shoot. However instead of telling Yudhistir to shoot, Guru Drona asked.

"What do you see Yudhistir?"

"Guruji, I can see the bird, the tree, the sky above and also the birds flying in the sky!" replied Yudhistir.

On hearing the answer Guru Drona told Yudhistir not to shoot and step aside.

Thereafter came one by one all the other princes to take the test. Guru Drona asked each of them the same question, but no one had anything different for an answer. Guru Drona kept telling all of them not to shoot and step aside. Meanwhile he started feeling dejected, until it was Arjuna's turn to take the test.

Arjuna came to the designated spot, stood in the upright position, lifted his bow, loaded the arrow, stretched the bowstring to his ears and took aim – ready to shoot.

Guru Drona repeated his question.

"What do you see, Arjuna?"

"The Eye"

"Shoot!" said immediately a delighted and a much-relieved Guru. The arrow zoomed past to hit the bird in its eye.

We have known this famous story for ages, but how many of us can claim to have learnt the inherent lesson.

How many of us can refine our focus to an extent where we become capable of seeing the 'eye' and nothing but the 'eye'.

The term 'planning' has been defined in a number of ways by a number of experts. However, I choose to call it the process which can help us refine our focus to an extent, where we become capable of seeing the *'eye'* and nothing but the *'eye'*.

Further, planning is not a one-time, stand-alone exercise. Instead it is very much part of a continuous chain of processes. Every plan must be followed by action, which in turn must be followed by a feedback. This feedback should be used to further fine-tune the plan. Thus in business context, planning is about five things in totality:

1. Setting up a target.
2. Designing a road-map to achieve the target.
3. Self-assessing the performance.
4. Refining the approach based on actual performance.
5. Continue working in light of this new understanding to achieve the target.

Before we start talking about how to develop a perfect business plan, let's discuss a few practical aspects associated with the process of business planning in general.

Why should I write my Business Plan?

Taking a lead from the above story, it might be recalled that not all of us are born with the ability to focus on our aim the way Arjuna could focus on his. The question is that if we are not born with the ability to focus like Arjuna then how can we learn it?

In context of business management this focus can be achieved through writing down our business plans?

Incidentally, way back in 1999, as part of one of my initial consultancy assignments for a dot.com client, we had conducted a survey on small-sized first generation entrepreneurs less than thirty five years of age. An interesting outcome of the survey was that as many as eighty two per cent of respondents felt that every entrepreneur must write down and properly document the Business Plan. However only eight per cent had actually done it for their own ventures. Further, we discovered that most of the respondents who had prepared a written business plan, had done it largely for meeting the statutory obligations of their financing agencies.

Why didn't these people prepare a written business plan? Most of the above respondents cited one or more of the following five reasons:

1. Our business is too small. What to write? Everything can be recalled on fingertips!
2. Our market is highly volatile; it keeps changing so often that there is no point in writing anything down.
3. We are sure of our success; so why unnecessarily write anything down and waste time.
4. It would simply be an academic exercise. What practical use does it have anyway.
5. How can we project what our sales or revenue are going to be; it could be simply anything. So what to write.

Each of the above reasons has some weight, but not heavy enough to scrap the advantage offered by a written business plan. No matter how big or small be the scale of operation, every entrepreneur must write his/her business plan. A written business plan, even a very simple one offers two distinct advantages to every budding entrepreneur.

1. It helps them scale down the overall ambiguity associated with the venture.
2. It provides specific benchmarks to assess actual performance over a period of time.

Successful entrepreneurs are realistic people, who live and work in real time and space. They are fully aware of their circumstances (positives as well as negatives). They visualize their initiatives to the finest of details and feel responsible for their actions. They don't procrastinate or leave things to chance. In other words they are the people who become capable of seeing the *'eye'* and nothing but the *'eye'*.

How Big Should Be the Written Business Plan?

Five years ago, while planning one of my ventures, I had got myself a book from the library. The title was – 'How to Write a Perfect Business Plan?' Following the instructions in the book, over the next 15 days, I prepared a hefty 40-page report – the perfect business plan!

Extremely satisfied with my own performance, I immediately congratulated myself for the effort and launched the venture. Over the next 20 months, the time my venture took to fail, two things kept happening simultaneously.

a. The hefty report kept lying quietly in one corner of my cupboard gathering dust all the time.
b. Subsequently, I found that nothing had gone as per what I had originally written in that hefty report.

Although this is an individual example, but isn't it something very common with a lot of us? We love to make plans, really big plans only to see them fizzle out at the execution stage. The question is how can we break this habit? How can we make plans that we feel capable of carrying out till the very end? Well, I can suggest a simple technique, which is as follows:

While planing my present venture I didn't want to commit the mistake I had committed the first time. I didn't want my plan to be a mere academic or decorative exercise. I wanted it to be a guiding document for my business. I wanted it to be in a format that could be used on a day-to-day basis. I wanted a structure that could help me evaluate my performance on a regular basis.

Unfortunately, I didn't know of any established technique to keep things small, simple, accessible and yet effective. So I used a little common sense and devised one of my own. Here is how I did it.

I took a blank diary and on the first page wrote the following three questions, to which I had written some very marginal answers:

- What do I want to do?
- How?
- How much revenue is it likely to generate?

I decided to persist with these three questions for three months before coming back to add more pages to the diary.

Interestingly over this period of three months I did manage some success with what I had wanted to do. In the sense, I managed to register a client and my 'accounts receivable' showed an entry of Rs.7000. Although a marginal amount, not bad for a start. Further, I had overshot my revenue target by twenty per cent.

Encouraged by the good response to the first plan I added another sheet for the next three months. This time I refined my questioning a little further and added a few more questions to the plan...

- What Business am I in?
- Who are my target customers?
- What are their needs?
- How am I reaching out to them?
- Why would they want to do business with me?
- What revenue can I expect to generate?

I continue with my diary even today. The only difference is that now I plan for an entire year and my plan include details on almost all issues related to my business.

In a nutshell, **the objective of writing the business plan should not be to prepare a hefty business report, but to evolve as an efficient business planner.**

Thus anything that helps you reduce the overall ambiguity associated with your business and provides you with a realistic benchmark to map your performance over a definite period of time is good to begin with. Ideally speaking – **start small, execute well and evolve bigger.**

Designing the Business Plan

In order to write down a detailed and elaborate plan for starting a new business, we must break down the entire process into three distinct steps.

Step 1. Identifying the Objectives
Step 2. Designing the Road Map
Step 3. Blocking the Loopholes

Henceforth we would go through the three steps one at a time in a systematic manner and learn to evolve a complete business plan.

The First Step – Identifying the Objectives

At the outset, every entrepreneur must define his/her business objectives at four levels:
- Immediate Objective (up to one years)
- Short-term Objective (two-three years)
- Mid-term Objective (five-seven years)
- Long-term Objective (ten-fifteen years)

Please remember that the objectives we define for ourselves must be realistic, achievable and yet progressive. I fully agree that it's something easier said than done. The question might arise in the minds of the readers at this stage that how to identify the objectives which are realistic, achievable and yet progressive, all at the same time? Let's learn it from those who have done it before us.

Here we shall discuss two cases portraying two diverse sets of objectives. Our first example is the case of Suresh Kumar and Dileep Kumar, the promoters of Imtech Industries, Trivandrum. Please recall that we had discussed the same case in the previous chapter under the heading 'Making the right choice – An anecdote'. We continue with the same example here also.

When Suresh and Dileep had started their venture in mid-1998, their **immediate objective** was to build a prototype machine and put it for demonstration at the Print-Pack Exhibition, New Delhi (Feb 1999). Thereafter their target was to keep assembling and selling one machine per month for the next two years. Simultaneously they wanted to bring their product at par with the best in the industry (**Short-term Objective**).

Their **mid-term objective** was to have a national level presence and build a company dealing in a wide range of machines/products used in the printing and binding industry. At the moment, they have offices in all five metros of the country. A year back, they took national distributorship of a well-known brand of adhesive, used in perfect binding machines – the product their company manufactures.

I don't know what their **long-term objective** or for that matter their **vision** is, as they have never disclosed it either to me or to anyone else. But in turn they have promised to invite me to a holiday at their would-be private resort on some secluded island somewhere deep in some ocean... some day!

Suresh and Dileep present a perfect case for those entrepreneurs who have great ambitions and who know how to fulfill those ambitions in a step-by-step manner.

Our second example is of Gopal Sharma, a thirty two year old accidental-entrepreneur from Bhopal, whom I had met some time back during a train journey. I am grateful to Gopal for sharing his experience with me.

Gopal, a postgraduate in sociology, had been jobless for nearly three years. Unable to find proper employment, he decided to start a travel agency along with his younger brother. His **immediate objective** was to end the tenure of unemployment and generate work for himself and his brother. With absolutely no prior experience in that type of work and hardly any capital to invest, he decided to start with something as mundane as Railway Ticketing. A table, a telephone and a pager were all he needed to start this venture from the portico in his house.

He confessed that he had no big ideas or plans at the time of starting the business, nor has he even now. All that he wanted to do was to continue ensuring a source of living and a comfortable life for himself and his family. Today, five years after the humble beginning his establishment employs three more people besides him and his brother. He has moved his office from the portico to a nearby commercial complex. His clientele includes a large number of individual as well as corporate clients of the locality. He offers a number of value-added services, besides the mundane Railway Ticketing services he had started five years ago.

Gopal's case presents a scenario in complete contrast with that of Suresh and Dileep. Gopal is a type of self-employed professional who has practically no great plans as to how he wants to grow his business. Besides he has no great expectations or ambitions from his venture. He is content with what he has been able to achieve so far and just wishes to consolidate on the same. He plans to continue working with the same dedication and take life as it comes to him, one day at a time.

On the other hand, Suresh and Dileep want to continue building upon on whatever they have been able to achieve till now. They have an ambition to move ahead and join the best and the biggest of their league and they seem to be working aggressively towards this big dream of theirs.

So what does that boil down to?

At the outset, it is difficult to say which of the two is more correct, because both are equally correct in their own context. Whereas Suresh and Dileep had got into the business to realize a dream, Gopal and his brother had logged on to self-employment to earn a source of living. Suresh and Dileep continue to pursue their dream, while Gopal and his brother continue to earn a living for themselves. Both these groups of people have been honest to their chosen purpose and thus have been able to draw realistic, achievable and yet progressive objectives for themselves at every stage and thus have excelled in their respective businesses.

The first requirement towards drawing realistic, achievable and yet progressive objectives is to be absolutely honest to one's chosen purpose. Thus once again ask yourself:

Why have I logged on to self-employment?

What do I expect to achieve from this venture?

Do I have sufficient resources to achieve the above?

The answer to the above questions would automatically lead you to realistic, achievable and yet progressive objectives best suited for your business. As said earlier also, there can't be any pre-prescribed answer to the above question. The correct answer is the one which you feel is appropriate for you. Please remember that this is a profession where you have to set your own targets, you have to define your own objectives and then you have to work to achieve those targets and get to your objectives. If you feel something is achievable, then it surely is. Thus the only way to ensure that you get the right answer to the above questions is by being honest to yourself.

I agree that despite all this commentary it might still not be easy for everybody to draw realistic, achievable and yet progressive objectives at the outset. If that were the case with you too, then just remember the old rule of entrepreneurship, which says:

"No problem in starting with what you have, provided you work to get what you should have."

So have faith in your ability to learn and get going with whatever you can manage at the moment. Just be honest to your chosen purpose and the rest would simply follow.

This brings us to the end of this chapter. Let's summarize what we have been discussing here.

Five Points to Remember

1. The objective of writing the business plan should not be to prepare a hefty business report, but to evolve as an efficient business planner.
2. A written business plan, even a very simple one, offers two distinct advantages to every budding entrepreneur.
    a. It helps them scale down the overall ambiguity associated with the venture.
    b. It provides specific benchmarks to assess actual performance over a period of time.
3. The process of planning can be divided into three distinct steps:
    a. Identifying the Objectives
    b. Designing the Road Map
    c. Blocking the Loopholes

4. The first step – Identifying the Objectives: Every entrepreneur must define his/her business objectives at four levels:
   a. Immediate Objective (up to one year)
   b. Short-term Objective (two-three years)
   c. Mid-term Objective (five-seven years)
   d. Long-term Objective (ten-fifteen years)
5. The questions that can help us draw realistic, achievable and yet progressive objective with reference to our venture are:
   a. Why have I logged on to self-employment?
   b. What do I expect to achieve from this venture?
   c. Do I have sufficient resources to achieve the above?

In the next chapter we discuss how to draw a road map to achieve the objectives we have set for ourselves here in this chapter.

5

Designing the Road Map

'I always like to look on the optimistic side of life, but I am realistic enough to know that life is a complex matter.'

Walt Disney

As mentioned in the previous chapter, we had divided the process of planning into three basic steps:

Step 1. Identifying the Objectives

Step 2. Designing the Road Map

Step 3. Blocking the Loop Holes

We have already discussed Step 1 in the previous chapter. In this chapter we shall discuss the second step of the planning process – 'Designing the Road Map'. Our discussion shall revolve around the following five basic functional domains that constitute an essential part of every business venture:

A. Sales and Marketing
   Customers, Competitors, Channel Partners
B. Production and/or Procurement
   Production Issues, Suppliers
C. Personnel and Administration
   Employees, General Administration, Choice of Business
      Partners
D. Statutory Obligations
   Nature of Business Entity, Laws of the land
E. Finance
   Raising Capital and Assessing Viability

Our approach shall be simple – we would be asking questions, till none remained unanswered. Please remember that our objective is not to prepare any hefty business report, but to evolve as an effective business planner.

Secondly, although the list of questions listed here is quite extensive, yet it is just for the purpose of providing an indicative guideline. As an entrepreneur you must add your own questions to the list, based on your perception of your would-be business. The more intense your questioning becomes, better would be your understanding about your business and its requirements.

In any case if you are not able to write answers to some or any of the questions mentioned below OR if you are not able to generate more questions to add to the list... don't quit! Instead just persist! Conduct some research. Go out into the market. Talk to your prospective customers. Talk to your competitor's customers. Talk to your competitors pretending to be their customer. Read more about your product/industry... and very soon the answers you need shall start appearing. Please remember, no one gets it all right at the first go, but those who persist, definitely get it right in due course of time.

Sales and Marketing

This functional area could be further divided into three sub-categories, viz., Customers, Competitors and Channel Partners.

Customers

No customer means: No Business! Hence our first question should be:

Who are my target customers?

Followed by...

Why would they buy what I have to offer?

How big is this target group?

Is this target group big enough to get me to my objective?

What price would they be willing to pay?

What would be the expected sales volumes? (Per day, per month, etc.)

How often would these people buy? (Repeat purchase rate)

Would all my sales be cash sales or would there be credit sales as well?

What are the terms of credit prevalent in the market? (Time of payment, interest, etc.)

How do I plan to communicate with my target customers? (Marketing Communication*)

---

* Marketing Communication primarily involves informing your target customers about your presence in the market. It could be through advertisements (Newspaper, Billboards, Radio, TV etc.), publicity campaigns, road shows, promotional events, personal meetings, etc. Further the medium of communication would have to be chosen depending on the nature of business and amount of resources available to you.

How do I wish to sell? What's my marketing strategy?
What would be my USP (Unique Selling Proposition)?
Why would the target group prefer to buy from me and
not from my competitors?
Why would a customer want to come back to me again?
Who all could be my first ten customers?

Competitors

You can hate them, but you can't neglect them!

Doesn't matter which industry you operate in, doesn't
matter how big or small be your venture, doesn't matter how
obscure might be your business, doesn't matter even if you
are a pioneer in your segment, no matter how you might be
placed in the marketing matrix, you are sure to have someone
running alongside, eyeing the same piece of cake, which you
desire to have. Welcome to the mad rush! The only way to
survive here is to stay constantly informed.

Ask Yourself:

Who are my competitors?
Who could be my competitors? (Suppliers of substitute
products/services)
What are they offering?
How is it different from what I am offering?
How much business are they doing?
How long have they been in business?
How do they sell?
How do they communicate with the customers?
Would their customers want to do business with me? If
yes, How?

What segment of their customers might want to do business with me?

Why their customers might **not** want to do business with me?

What competitive advantage do I enjoy over them?

What competitive advantage do they enjoy over me?

What's the overall market scenario?

How's the general state of business?

How long can I retain my competitive advantage?

How would I be required to change with time?

Channel Partners

Several businesses require our product/services to go through a number of people before reaching the end customer. These intermediate people could be our distributors, stockists, agents, associates, etc. Although they do not form part of our enterprise, but still our success might depend to a great extent on their performance and their level of commitment to our product or service. Hence we must be extra careful in choosing the right kind of people.

Ask Yourself:

Do I need any channel partners to run my business?

What do I need them for?

What responsibilities would I want them to carry out?

What would be my liabilities in return?

What kind of channel partners do my competitors have?

How are my competitors managing their channel partners?

Can a similar arrangement offer me the best-value proposition?

If not, then what changes would make the relationship more effective for my venture?

At times it might not be possible for first-generation entrepreneurs to get associated with the best players in the market. In such cases, use your judgment and choose the best out of what is available to you.

Managing channel partner relationship might be very critical for certain kind of businesses, e.g. production or manufacturing based businesses, where you essentially need people to take your products to the market.

It is advised that if you don't have sufficient experience or knowledge of managing these relationships, invest some time in your education. Believe me these relationships are not always as simple as they might appear to be from the outside! A little extra effort at this stage might prove worthwhile later.

Production and Procurement

This functional area could be divided into two categories, viz., Production Issues and Suppliers.

Production Issues

At the outset let me confess that I hardly have any experience of managing industrial production of any kind. Whatever I know has been through my interactions with friends and colleagues, who have been involved with different types of manufacturing activities.

Although I don't have any industrial background, I have been involved with other kinds of developmental projects. These have been things like web development, content development, database development, etc. Somehow I have come to realize that the basic issues under both the environments remain predominantly the same. I have used this experience of mine to design questions for this particular segment. Please make amendments as per your needs and requirements.

To plan on this front, ask Yourself:

What are the best practices prevalent in the industry? (technology, skills, etc.)

Can I afford the best?

If Yes, Am I capable enough to manage the best?

If No, What can I afford at the moment?

How much would it cost?

How long would it take me to graduate to the best?

What's my plan to graduate to the best?

For the time being, how can I derive the best out of what I can afford?

How is it likely to affect my performance in the market?

Can some of the production/developmental activities/processes be outsourced?

What would be the comparative cost equation in such cases? (Outsourcing vs. In-house production)

Would quality be ensured if the activity is outsourced?

What technological developments are taking place in my industry?

What technological developments are taking place in industries relevant to my business?

What changes are likely to emerge in the due course of time?

How can I get ready for these expected changes?

Every entrepreneur might not be in a position to afford the best piece of plant and machinery, equipment, technology, etc. from they very outset. Most of the times, top of the line stuff demands big investment and a first-time entrepreneur might not have enough financial leverage to afford the best. On such occasions, it is mostly the entrepreneur's personal resolve to keep growing that keeps him/her going. A possible option is to find creative and innovative solutions to advance.

Suppliers

These are the people who form the back-end of our business. For example: for a manufacturing/production company they could be the suppliers of raw material, accessories, components, etc. For other kind of businesses (e.g. retail, etc.) they could be suppliers of finished goods for sale (distributors, whole-sellers, agents, stockists from whom we would buy).

Ask Yourself:

What would I need suppliers for?
Who are the three best suppliers in the market?
How do they sell?
What are their terms of sale?
How reliable are their services?
What levels of inventory would I be required to maintain?
How frequently would I be required to purchase from my suppliers?
What kind of competition exists in their segment/industry?
What kind of services are they offering to my competitors?

Two elementary rules for choosing your suppliers:

1. Never take things on their face value; always question the obvious.

2. Never lay all your eggs in the same basket. Keep multiple sources of supply.

You must choose suppliers who can help you deliver the best value to your customers and thus help you optimize your returns. A little effort in this direction at the beginning could save you a lot of trouble afterwards.

Personnel and Administration

This functional area could be divided into three segments, viz., Employees, General Administration and Choice of Partners.

Employees

You might need some people to help you run your business. You should be aware of your manpower needs from the very beginning.

Ask Yourself:

What work functions am I going to perform myself? (Those entering Partnership businesses should define job-profile of each partner distinctly.)
Where do I need help from others?
How many people would I need?
What role is each of them going to play?
What Qualities, Qualification and Skills must they possess?
How much am I ready to pay them?
What is the prevailing market standard for emoluments?
What would be my other liabilities as an employer? (PF, group-insurance, etc.)

What cost-benefit ratio do I derive from the exercise?
Can a part-time employee do the same job?
Can the work be outsourced?

My only suggestion on this front is that you must hire the best possible talent, under the given circumstances. Once selected, take good care of your people. Be a responsible employer, a community otherwise found rarely in our country especially amongst small businesses.

General Administration

Ask Yourself:

What infrastructure do I need to run my operations?
(Business Premises, Office Equipment, Furniture, Office Stationery, Vehicles, etc.)
How much would each of the above cost?
What other running expenses would I be incurring?
(Telephone Bills, Electricity, ISP charges, petty office expenses, etc.)
...and related issues

Over the last ten years the concept of **home-office** has emerged very strongly across the world. A large number of small as well as large entrepreneurs operate from their home-offices, running almost all kinds of business ventures. From the point of view of convenience and costs, home-offices are simply great. See if a similar arrangement could work in your case.

The only point to remember is that an entrepreneur operating from the home-office would always have to enforce strict self-discipline to keep his/her personal commitments away from the professional ones.

Choice of Business Partners

Business Partners could be of two types:
1. Internal (Relevant for Partnership firms)
2. External (Relevant for Franchising, Distributorship, Agency type businesses)

Let's discuss each of them separately.

Internal Business Partners: Entrepreneurs wanting to enter business in partnership with someone else always face the question—Who to Choose as a Partner?

Ask Yourself:

Do I have the temperament to be a partner? (Some people are actually better off alone)

What do I need a partner for? (Funds, technical skills, marketing, etc.)

Who could be my prospective partner?

Can we work with each other in harmony?

Can we share similar business objectives and vision?

Do we bring together complementary skills to the venture?

Choose a person with whom you can share similar objectives. These objectives should not only be in terms of professional achievements but also in terms of personal growth and ambitions. The two of you should be able to work as a team, collectively trying to focus on the same target.

Historically speaking people with complementary skills or personalities have made for some of the most successful partnership businesses of all times (e.g. Rolls and Royce). Well, you could be the next, provided you choose the right kind of person as a partner.

External Business Partners: This is primarily applicable for franchising, distributorship, agency, and loan-licence type of businesses. So in case you are entering any of the above type of business,

Ask Yourself:

Does the parent company's business proposition match with my business objectives?
Does the parent company's business philosophy go in line with the values I believe in?

How good has been the company's track record?
What has been the state of their business and industry?
How have they been performing?

What do other franchisees have to say about their experience with the company?
How well have these people been doing?
What training and marketing support does the company propose to provide?

The success of McDonalds and KFC worldwide has made franchising a popular kind of business model for both franchisers as well as franchisees. However, all that glitters is not gold. Entrepreneurs must join hands with brands/companies that have shown to possess a consistent track record and display a commitment for mutual growth.

Statutory Obligations

This functional area could be classified into two categories, viz., Nature of Business Entity and Laws of the land – The Government.

Nature of Business Entity

There are four types of legally permissible business entities:

1. Public Limited Company – Usually a business form recommended for large businesses. A public limited company can invite members of the public to subscribe to its shares, which are subsequently openly traded in a stock exchange. These companies are subjected to several statutory requirements under the Companies Act.

2. Private Limited Company – This is a limited liability company, where an entrepreneur's liability is limited to the amount of money contributed by the way of share capital. Private limited companies are incorporated in accordance with the provisions given in the Companies Act and are subjected to compliance under the same. The number of shareholders in such companies cannot exceed fifty, with a minimum of at least three.

3. Partnership Firm – As the name suggests, a firm owned by two or more persons, joined together through a partnership agreement/deed is a partnership firm. The partners jointly reap the rewards and bear the risks of the business. The legal regulations governing these firms are set out in the Partnership Act.

4. Proprietorship Firm – This is a firm, which is started by a sole person as its owner. The promoter of such an entity solely enjoys the rewards and assumes the risks of the business.

Ideally an accidental entrepreneur must start his/her business as a proprietorship firm or at the most as a partnership firm. These type of business entities are easy to start, simple to run and under worst circumstances comparatively hassle free to close. Once well established, a move towards the higher grade could be made within no time. The other business entities require greater number of statutory obligations and regulatory expenses.

Laws of the land – The Government

In case you are wondering what the government might have to do with your business, well then I suggest you change your notions fast. You would need to interact with the government at all levels as long as you are interested in operating a legal business.

So ask Yourself:

Would my business require any licenses/Govt. clearances/registration, etc.?
If yes, How do I plan to get them?
How long does it take to get these clearances?
What would be the cost?

What tax liabilities would the business be incurring?
Indirect taxes: Customs, Excise and Sales Tax
Direct taxes: Corporate/Personal Income Tax

What bookkeeping norms would I be required to follow?

How frequently would these statutory obligations arise? What external support would I need to complete the obligations? (CA, lawyers, etc.)

There is a tendency among young entrepreneurs to shy away from this aspect of their business and often leave all affairs to be handled only when it becomes obligatory. Lack of proper knowledge leads them to waste valuable time and money in unnecessary fire-fighting operations, often at the mercy of wrong kind of people. Hence investigate the details on this front before you take a plunge into the water.

Finance

In case your knowledge about the financial-technicalities of running a business needs replenishment, I suggest you read the book: Finance Sense – An easy guide for non-finance executives, by Prasanna Chandra. It shall give you a good foundation to begin with.

Under this heading we shall talk about issues like how to identify your investment needs, raise the necessary capital and assess preliminary viability of the project. So let's begin...

Raising Capital

Ask Yourself:

How much money do I need to start the business?
How much would be the initial investment?
What would be the recurring expenditure?
What options do I have for raising this amount?
How much can I raise through Equity? (Investment)
How much can I raise through Debt? (Loan)
What would be the expected cash-inflows?

Would the expected cash inflows from the business be sufficient:

- To allow me service the debt
- To allow me take care of the operational expenses
- To leave some surplus for the equity partners (Prepare a cash-flow statement)

How much time should it take me to break-even*?

Does it sound to be a viable business proposition?

It might not be easy for accidental entrepreneurs to raise money from banks, financial institutions or for that matter venture capitalists under normal circumstances. Most of these financing agencies look for the past record of the promoter, where accidental entrepreneurs might not have much to display. Therefore under most cases accidental entrepreneurs would have to rely initially either on self generated capital or on private loans from family or friends.

---

* Break-even point: What is it? It is the point where your accumulated profits exceed your total investment in the business. In other words, the point when you recoup all your investment from the business. For example, say you start your venture with a capital of Rs.50,000 and infuse no further capital from your side thereafter, then you break-even the day your accumulated profits reach the figure of Rs.50,000.

Breaking-even means you are now ready to do business with the money you generate out of the venture. In other words you would have pulled out all your money from the business. Later, in Chapter 8 we shall discuss the concept of 'doing business with other people's money', which shall make things more clear.

Incidentally, banks do provide some conditional funding under Prime Minister's Rozgar Yojana (PMRY) to unemployed youths for setting up their own ventures.*

Besides, Small Industries Development Bank of India (SIDBI) (*www.sidbi.com*) has a number of direct and indirect financing schemes for small entrepreneurs, including micro-credit options for projects in rural and semi-rural areas.

In reference to external financing, one question that haunts all entrepreneurs alike is:

What do financing agencies look for before extending finance to venture?

Every financing agency is primarily interested in two things, viz., earning an interest and getting their money back safely. Thus they ask entrepreneurs about two things:

a. ROC (Return on Capital) expected from the project.

b. USP (Unique Selling Proposition) of the project.

Anyhow financing agencies are more likely to support conservative projects with steady revenue streams rather than hyper-ambitious dream projects with highly uncertain streams. And as said earlier people with a successful track record are more likely to receive big money than the ones without.

Over the last decade a new breed of investors have surfaced on to the entrepreneurial scenario. These are the people called Venture Capitalists (VCs) and also Angel Investors. Venture Capitalists are the people who are in the

---

*   Details available at *www.ssi.nic.in/schpmry.html* or contact your banker.

business of investing in up-start ventures and are willing to take greater amounts of risk.*

Let's consolidate

After having come along this much, we should have answers to the following questions:

The beginning...

What Business am I in? (Chapter 2)
What are my Business Objectives? (Chapter 4)

Sales and Marketing

Who are my target customers?
How do I plan to sell to them?
What are my immediate sales targets?
How much revenue am I targeting to generate?

Production and/or Procurement

How do I plan to manage my internal processes?
What shall be my investment in building the infrastructure and running the operations?

Personnel and Administration

How do I plan to run the administration?
What shall be my various cost-centres?

Statutory Obligations

Have I clearly identified all the statutory obligations associated with my business?

---

* The website *www.ecomready.net* offers some valuable resources on Venture Capital funding in India.

What costs would I be incurring on this front?

Finance

Does it sound to be a viable business proposition?
How do I plan to raise the necessary capital?

And finally...

What factors would help me achieve my objectives?
  Internal
  External
What factors would work against me?
  Internal
  External

The answers to these questions would serve as the basic framework of our business plan. However, no plan can be called foolproof unless it has been meticulously checked for any possible loopholes and that is what we do in our next chapter. In our next chapter we check our business plan for any possible loopholes, besides also designing a contingency plan to take care of any eventualities.

6

Blocking the Loopholes

'Only one thing is certain – that is, nothing is certain.
If this statement is true, it is also false.'

An Ancient Paradox

In this chapter we shall discuss the final step of the process of designing a Business Plan. We have already discussed Step 1 – 'Identifying the Objectives' and Step 2 – 'Designing the Road Map' over the previous two chapters. In this chapter we would first self-test our Road Map for any possible loopholes and then would design a contingency plan to be ready for any adverse eventuality, besides discussing a few other independent issues that might hold relevance for budding entrepreneurs at this stage. In all we discuss the following in this chapter:

1. How foolproof is my Road Map?
2. Summarizing the Business Plan
3. How to exit, if I fail?

4. Preparing a Contingency Plan
5. The 'Business Plan' Competitions
6. Weakness Entrepreneurs Possess

How foolproof is My Road Map?

We had ended the previous chapter with what we called the basic framework of our business plan. Now it's time to rock the equilibrium. In this section we shall self-test our framework for any possible loopholes before taking it to the implementation stage. The question might be—how do we self-test the viability of our self-drawn objectives and our self-designed Road Map? The answer is, we once again utilize to our benefit –*'the positive power of negative thinking'*

However, before we begin, I would like to call your attention towards an essential point that must be addressed at this stage.

Please keep in mind that this exercise must be conducted at least a few days after you have designed your Road Map. Don't perform it immediately after completing the Step 2. *Necessarily allow some time (at least a couple of days) between the two steps*. This time gap would help you get out of the stream of optimistic thoughts that might be flowing through your mind while conceptualizing Step 1 and Step 2, and would help you take a realistic view of the overall scenario.

Once ready, begin by asking Yourself...

What would happen if I fail?

Under what circumstances could I possibly fail? (External Threats)

How can I survive these adverse circumstances?
What's my plan to be ready for the worst?

What weak-links in my plan can lead me to failure?
(Internal Weaknesses)
How can I turn these weaknesses into strengths?
What's my plan to convert these weaknesses into strengths?

What are the things about my business that I don't know yet? (Personal Weaknesses)
What's my plan to learn what I don't know yet?
How ready am I to be an entrepreneur?

What is it that's still incomplete or missing in my plan?
What's my plan to complete it?

Once through with the general questioning, get specific...

What can stop me from achieving my:
• Immediate Objectives
• Short-term Objectives
• Mid-term Objectives
• Long-term Objectives

Have I identified my target customers correctly?
What can stop my target customers from coming to me?
What competitive forces can stop me from getting established?
What market conditions can force me out of business?
What can stop me from delivering the best value proposition to my customers?
What can stop me from raising adequate capital?

What can prevent me from utilizing optimally the raised capital?

What legal/procedural hurdles might slow down my progress?

What personal attributes could make me lose interest in the business?

What am I most afraid of at the moment?

What's adding to my anxiety?

...Keep asking questions till you have removed all your doubts, fears and anxieties. Keep asking till no question remains unanswered. Make necessary amendments/adjustments to your 'Road-Map' (Previous Chapter) based on what new answers you discover here at this stage.

This exercise might sound boring or unnecessary to some of the readers. But let me assure you that it is neither. You would discover its usefulness only much later at the time of running your venture. It is a sort of fire prevention exercise, which lets you spot the potential possibilities that could start a fire and accordingly help you make arrangements to safeguard against them much in advance. Otherwise at a later stage you might just end up spending most of your time managing fire-fighting operations rather than working to grow your business.

Summarizing the Business Plan

So far we have gone through the following three steps:

    a. We identified our business objectives (Chapter 4)

    b. We designed a Road Map to achieve the above objectives (Chapter 5)

    c. We tried to locate the loopholes, if any, in our Road Map (running chapter)

By now you would have all the relevant information about every aspect associated with your prospective venture. Besides, most of you would know instinctively by now how to arrange this newly acquired information to develop a successful business venture. But once again, being the author, it is my responsibility to explain how to consolidate these findings and summarize it into what might be called a Perfect Business Plan.

This Perfect Business Plan is nothing but simple compilation of the acquired information under a meaningful structure that could be used by us at all times. Here I am suggesting an orthodox structure, which I had learned from one of the computer programmes and which I have been using for my venture. However, you are free to assemble this information any way you like. Please remember, our mission is to establish a successful business venture. Hence anything that helps us accomplish our mission would be good enough.

Please fill the necessary information, which you would have acquired by going through Steps 1,2 and 3, under the following heading and related sub-headings. As said earlier also, feel free to add/modify the headings as per the needs of your business or your personal preferences. This is just an indicative structure.

THE COMPLETE BUSINESS PLAN

Business/Company Background

Desired Positioning
Competitive Advantage

Market Overview

Target Market Description
Purchase Criteria
Target Market Growth Rate

Product Overview

Product/Service
Pricing
Expected Revenue

Business Strategy

Marketing Plan
(Marketing channels, selling, value addition, customer relation, etc.)
Team
Opportunities
Competition
Risks
Investment

Funding Structure

Timeline of Events

Financial Statements

Budgets, Cash Flow, Projected Profit and Loss Statement, etc.

Special Comments (if any)

After having finally designed a perfect business plan, it is time for us to decide upon one more important issue at this stage.

So just ask Yourself...

When do I plan to conduct a comprehensive Audit of my business?

How do I plan to keep monitoring my progress on a regular basis?

And finally, before we close this subject and move on to the next topic, we must remind ourselves about something we shall be chasing all the time, i.e. our targets! So refresh your memory and list somewhere exclusively the answer to the following question.

What are my targets for the immediate Audit period? Targets in terms of–
- Achievement of Business Objectives
- Sales Target
- Revenue Target
- Market Coverage
- Technology Adoption, etc.

Define your targets and get set to move ahead.

How to exit, if I fail?

The ancient wisdom says, 'Hope for the best, but stay prepared for the worst!' So after having planned for the best, let's get ready even for the worst.

This is essential because several businesses require certain formalities to be completed before they can be actually closed down in the legal sense. Besides, a little investigation over this front would introduce you to a totally untouched dimension of your proposed business, which shall in the end help you take an informed decision.

Most of the exit-obligations arise on two fronts.

a. Financial Obligations (Repayment of Bank loans, Trade creditors, Employees, etc.)
b. Statutory Legal Obligations (Cancellation of Tax Registration, Licenses, Permits, etc.)

Anyway, whatever be the nature of your business, you must find answers to the following questions at this stage:

What obligations would I be incurring if I have to close the venture?

How much time does it take to complete the formalities?

How much money would I need to spend over the exercise?

Would it be possible to sell the business to someone else?

What kind of person would like to buy such a business?

What would I look for in a business if I were to buy such a business?

...And so on.

Preparing a Contingency Plan

So far we have been contemplating failure, hoping that it would never happen in reality. However, what happens if we actually fail! It's time to get ready for that eventuality.

Ask Yourself:

What would I do if my venture actually fails?

What options would I have then?

What happens if I fail in six months time?

What happens if I fail in two years time?

What happens if I fail in five years time?

What happens if I fail in five to ten years time?

What kind of opportunities would I have at that time?

How would I be financially, socially and professionally placed at that time?

In what direction is my present experience expected to take me?

How useful would this experience be, while looking for a new opening?

Could my existing venture be transformed into something new at that time?

What possibilities would I retain as an entrepreneur?

No matter how frail and fragile the answers might appear at the moment, definitely map a few alternatives for yourself. Sometimes even by thinking exclusively in this direction, you could gain valuable insight about your existing business and on ways you would want to develop it. For example, I had never known myself to be a writer. Writing had never been my cup of tea. But then one day I asked myself,

What could I do if my business fails?

And from somewhere came the answer that maybe I could write a book on how NOT to run a business!

Thankfully, by God's grace, my business is doing reasonably well. Nevertheless I could still move ahead with that mundane idea of writing a book and could in turn visualize this book *Accidental Entrepreneur.* **Hence never underestimate the positive power of negative thinking.**

With this we come to the end of our discussion on how to build a perfect business plan for a new venture. However, this does not mean the end of this chapter. Before we close the chapter and also along with it the Planning Phase, I would like to highlight some bits of information that I feel could be interesting as well as useful for every budding entrepreneur.

Business Plan Competitions

I hope you already have at least heard about the 'Business Plan Competitions'. Over the recent years several leading educational institutes as well as corporate groups have been organizing 'business plan competitions' for budding entrepreneurs. The objective of these competitions is to help young people convert vague ideas into an innovative business proposition.

Winners of such competitions are awarded with hefty cash prizes. The panel of judges normally includes successful entrepreneurs, corporate bigwigs, academicians, bankers, venture capitalists, industry analysts, etc. Such competitions serve as an ideal gateway to young would-be entrepreneurs to have a guided interaction with the potential strategic collaborators and mentors.

Almost every major university in the developed world holds such competitions on an annual basis for its students. Several of these competitions are open to outsiders as well. The details are widely available over the web; just type "Business Plan Competition" into any search engine and you shall have an exhaustive list. In India, the two most popular competitions have been:

a. Eureka—The annual business plan competition organized by Entrepreneurship Cell, IIT Bombay (Mumbai). (*www.iitb.ac.in/~ecell/*)

b. I2I (Ideas To Implementation)—A Business plan competition organized by Entrepreneurship Cell, IIM Calcutta (Kolkata). (*www.iimcatalyst.com*)

Besides, there was **India Ventures 2000**, a competition organized by McKinsey and Company. I hope the company would re-launch a new addition in the coming years. Further, the ministry of Science and Technology in India has set-up a **National Innovation Foundation (NIF)** in collaboration with IIM Ahmedabad. NIF holds an annual contest for grassroots level innovations, innovative technologies and creative concepts supporting traditional knowledge. The details can be had from *www.nifindia.org* or *www.sristi.org*.

It's worthwhile to participate in these competitions as these events could serve as a great learning opportunity for every entrepreneur. Even if you don't win a prize, you would not come back as a loser. At the end of the day, you would have gained much more than what you would have invested into the exercise.

Weaknesses Entrepreneurs Possess

In the opening chapter of the book – 'Understanding the Basics' we had talked about the strengths successful entrepreneurs have shown to possess. We close this chapter by highlighting the weaknesses they have shown to possess in general. These are:

1. They establish unrealistic time frames.
2. They try to achieve too much too quickly.
3. They underestimate resources needed to achieve the goals.

4. They get over-optimistic about their business idea.
5. They fail to see the flip side of the business idea.
6. They attempt to accomplish too much alone.
7. They tend to be impulsive managers, which leads them in circles.
8. They get infatuated by a little initial success and lose focus.
9. They find it hard to delegate as the business grows.
10. They fail to develop an efficient second level of command.

Once again I let you decide how you are going to use this information to the best of your advantage!

What's Next!

After having talked about designing the business plan, it's now time to move on to the implementation stage. Well, that is what we do over the next three chapters.

Although there are several aspects related to the day-to-day running of a business, our focus shall remain centered on the question—*Where do entrepreneurs fail in executing their plans?*

Various surveys and researches have shown that while executing their plans, the entrepreneurs have mostly shown to fail at either one of the following three places:

1. They fail to establish a distinct identity for themselves in the market
2. They get entangled in managing the working capital necessities of the venture

3. They fail to develop a proper network to let the business grow on its own

Accordingly, we discuss each of the above issues over the next three chapters. For anything else, which you might need to know about running and managing a business, you could easily find excellent resources in specialized works of better known authors.

SECTION III

IMPLEMENTATION PHASE

7

Getting Established

'You are never given a wish without also being given the power to make it true. You may have to work for it, however.'

Richard Bach

In this chapter we discuss the following:
1. Anonymity – An entrepreneur's nightmare
2. Three Strategies to Entrepreneurial Success
   a. Come First – Move Fast – Grow Big
   b. If you can't beat them, join them!
   c. Your AGILITY is your only weapon
3. A blueprint for Accidental Entrepreneurs

Anonymity – An Entrepreneur's Nightmare

I don't know you
I don't know your company
I don't know your product

I don't know your customers
I don't know your background
I don't know your reputation
Now, what was it you wanted to sell me!

Selling indeed is a tough job and it's even tougher when you are representing a new or unknown entity. I am yet to come across an entrepreneur, who has not got kicked around or on whose face doors have not been slammed especially during those initial years in business. But then that's what the game is all about. That's what separates Men from the ordinary Boys – their ability to break out of the clutches of anonymity and create a distinct identity and get established in the crowded marketplace.

However the question might arise that, what exactly do we mean when we mention the two terms, viz., **Creating an Identity** and **Getting Established**? Let's learn it from a popular adventure of the legendary English hero – Robin Hood.

One day Robin Hood, who lived with his fellow men in the Sherwood Forest decided to visit Nottingham to get some news about what had been happening in the city. To be specific he was more interested to know what was going on in the Sheriff's mind, as the crooked fellow had been silent for quite sometime now.

He had an idea to find out the latest from Nottingham. He bought a lot of meat from a nearby hamlet and went to the big market of Nottingham pretending to be a butcher. It was the 'All Butcher's Day' and thus the market was jammed with butchers from all over. Robin was the only new face. Once in the market, Robin made a quick survey of what was happening around and settled down to trade.

Interestingly Robin Hood had no intentions of making any monetary profit out of the business; instead his interest was in grabbing attention of everyone around him. So he decided to sell his stuff at one-fifth the price of what other traders were selling in the market. He shouted from the top of his counter to let everyone know about his generous offer. The word spread fast and soon his counter was crowded with customers wanting to buy more.

Other butchers were suddenly gripped in panic, failing to understand what the young man, who had never been seen in the market before, had wanted to achieve from his actions. Some started calling him mad, while others labeled him a quack. Someone said he was selling cheap because his meat was foul. However none of this tattle could have any adverse effect on Robin's customers, who instead found the meat to be of excellent quality and the butcher to be nice, accommodative and humble.

Thus within no time, Robin Hood had sold off all his stuff and by noon everybody in the market was talking nothing else but only about him.

Creating an Identity is about drawing the attention of your target customers and attracting them towards your brand/business and **Getting Established** means reaching a position, where your customers as well as your competitors start treating you as a serious player in the market.

We don't run our businesses to incur a loss, but still this Robin Hood story can teach us some very important tips about what it takes to create a distinct identity and get established in the market. In brief it is about five things:

1. Having clear Objectives
2. Creating a Unique Selling Proposition
3. Generating Competitive Advantage
4. Communicating clearly with the Customers
5. Delivering what you promise

Further, let's learn the art from those who have done it successfully before us and accordingly design a blueprint best suited for our business.

Three Strategies to Entrepreneurial Success

Successful entrepreneurs in past have shown to follow one of the following three strategies to create an identity and get established in the market.

1. Come First – Move Fast – Grow Big
2. If you can't beat them, join them!
3. Your *Agility* is your only weapon

Let's discuss each in detail.

Come First – Move Fast – Grow Big

- Infosys
- Sehnaz Hussain's Herbal Products
- NDTV
- NIIT
- Talisma Corp.
- Hotmail.com
- Naukri.com
- Brilliant Tutorials
- Archies Cards
- Zee Network

What's common to all these entrepreneurial ventures? Perhaps the road they took to success! Let's see how?

1. Each of these ventures brought into the market, either...
   A new product line,
   or
   A new business concept,
   or
   A new commercial idea,
   or simply...
   A new way of doing the same old thing.

2. By doing this they became pioneers of a new category of business for which the market had till then not been explored and a little demand had already existed.

3. They ensured that these new solutions offered a better value to the customers compared to the substitutes available in the market.

4. Once in the market, these players moved aggressively and quickly to consolidate their first-mover's advantage and worked hard to generate tremendous brand value.

5. They focused on developing capabilities, which helped them create capacities to attain a leadership position in the market.

6. As a result, the big competition, which subsequently followed them into the market, could not shuffle them out because by then they had already got themselves well established.

7. Thereafter continuous reinvention has helped these enterprises retain their USP and their leadership position in the minds of their customers as well as in the market. This is a high risk – high return strategy, best suited for

entrepreneurs who come into the market riding an innovative business concept. However, for every entrepreneur who succeeds—there would have been several others who fail. It's definitely tough to keep leading the herd from the front at all times. Still new entrepreneurs keep jumping in; perhaps the expected rewards of anticipated success are too alluring to resist!

If you can't beat them, join them!

What would you do if you don't have an exceptional business idea that would set the markets on fire instantaneously? An option is to join hands with someone who has such an idea! In other words join hands with someone who has already proved to be a success in the market.

Example:

- You might not be in a position to start an automobile company, but you could set up an ancillary or could choose to become an authorized dealer of any leading automobile company.
- If you don't want to take the risk of starting a new restaurant, you could become a franchisee of a well-established chain of restaurants, etc.

Thus there are businesses of the following nature:
- Joint Ventures
- Marketing Alliances
- Strategic Alliances
- Franchising
- Ancillary Units
- Loan-license Manufacturing

- Agency
- Dealerships
- Channel Partners
- Distributors
- Marketing Agents
- Marketing Retainers
- Consultants, etc.

All the above types of businesses could be an association between two parties – An established parent company and an individual entrepreneur. From an entrepreneur's point of view this strategy offers following advantages:

1. The entrepreneur gets to execute his/her venture over a business model that has already been tested successfully in the market.
2. The entrepreneur gets to enjoy the benefits of the brand equity enjoyed by the parent company.
3. The entrepreneur gets to work in close association with the parent company, often receiving support in form of staff training, marketing inputs, national level advertising, etc. Thus bringing up the venture doesn't remain a lonely fight.
4. Besides, bankers and financial institutions love to finance such projects, provided the parent company enjoys a good footing in the market.

This strategy suits best two types of entrepreneurs:

1. Those who have a good amount of capital to invest.
2. Those who don't want to take the risk of bringing up a totally new enterprise.

Interestingly this is a mid-way option that allows entrepreneurs the thrill of running their own show and at the same time staying closely associated to an established name. David Coates in his book, *The Complete Entrepreneur*, calls such people – 'The half-way entrepreneurs'. Normally these types of businesses don't make entrepreneurs very rich very soon, but they start offering a steady stream of return within no time.

Your AGILITY is Your Only Weapon

So far we have talked about two types of people
a. Those who aim to be pioneers
b. Those who join the pioneers/leaders

However, what about those who neither have any revolutionary business idea nor do they wish to partner with someone who has one? What about people, who might be running one of the usual 'me-too' type businesses? How do such people create an identity and get established in the market? Let's look at some of the better known success stories:

- **Rajeev Samant,** a software engineer working with Oracle in Silicon Valley, decided to come home to India because he had a dream. His dream was to set up a vineyard and brew wine. So in 1997-98 he set up a company by the name of 'Sula Vineyards', with 30 acres of plantation near Nasik. 'Sula Vineyard' sold more than 10,000 cases in the year 2000-01. By doing this they have already joined the list of top five players in the market. Total market size for domestic wine in India is about 1,50,000 cases per year.

- 1997-98, a time when the global pizza giants like Pizza Hut, Dominos and Pizza Express were already getting well settled in India, **Antoina Bakhache** was negotiating with a venture capitalist in Geneva to get funding for his dream venture – **'Pizza Corner'** in India. Today Pizza Corner has around 25 outlets all over India. Bakhache wants to make Pizza Corner the best managed pizza chain in the world.

- In 1993-94 **Taab Sidiqqui** along with her husband started making bread under the brand name **'Harvest Gold'** from a small plant near Delhi. Initially people wouldn't take her product even for free, but things have changed drastically since then. Today, 'Harvest Gold' is the largest selling brand in and around Delhi, catering to a big proportion of the city's total bread demand. Perhaps what changed her fortunes were innovative packaging, good quality and her personal determination to succeed.

- **DS Narang** had started making herbal products at his home in Patel Nagar, Delhi. That was 10 years ago. Today he has six plants, over 1500 distributors, 20 odd C&F agents, a turnover of around Rs. 100 crore (US $ 20 million) and a well-known brand named **'Ayur'**. The secret behind his success, he says, is a quality product supplied at half the price his competitors sell for.

- In 1982, **MP Ramachandran** working as an accountant at a chemical trading company came across an idea and decided to get into the whitener business. He launched a company by the name of **Jyothi Laboratories** and named his brand **'Ujala'**. Today the Ujala brand controls more than 70 per cent of the Rs. 200 crore whitener market in the country. All these years Ramachandran's direct competition had been with world famous Reckitt-Benckiser & Co (brand name – Robin Blue). A good quality product, price competitiveness and some savvy marketing have been the three main reasons behind his success.

- Who could think of getting into the Toothpaste business, where global FMCG giants like HLL and Colgate-Palmolive rule the markets? Actually, **Atul Shah** did and came into the market with his **Anchor** brand toothpaste five years ago. He positioned 'Anchor' as the 100% vegetarian toothpaste and focused on the markets of Rajasthan and Gujarat, two pre-dominantly vegetarian states. Further, he offered a quality product at almost half the price his competitors were charging. Today **Anchor** is a Rs.150 crore brand and is placed number three after the two FMCG giants in the market.

The question is:
With nothing extraordinary to boast about, how would have these entrepreneurs established their identity and succeeded in the market? Let's analyze:

1. Such entrepreneurs enter a market, which is already fiercely competitive.
2. With no distinct USP to bank upon, they position themselves in relation to the existing order.
3. They move fast and get deep into action, using their resources to the optimum and making best of every given opportunity.

4. Continued perseverance allows them enough leverage to keep surviving through the initial start-up phase.

5. Further they use their agility to stay informed about the happening changes and emerging opportunities, ahead of their competition. They keep looking for an opening in the existing market order.

6. The moment they spot an opening, they aggressively move-in to create an USP and a leadership position in the market. For example, Atul Shah of 'Anchor' moved in with the concept of 100 per cent vegetarian toothpaste. A concept that had till then been alien to the two market leaders – HLL and Colgate Palmolive.

7. Thereupon they streamline their energies and consolidate their efforts in the direction of this new opening and thus emerge as an established player in the market.

A real-life example would help improve our understanding at this stage:

A friend and fellow entrepreneur, **Sharad Varshney,** now a seventh year veteran had started his career selling and servicing PCs for other dealers. Once equipped with some practical experience, he floated his outfit, a proprietorship company. For next two years he kept selling and servicing whatever he could lay his hands on. His technical competence, competitive prices, personalized service and a never-ending desire to help his customers saw him develop a good rapport in the market.

Those were mid-1990's, the Internet boom was just setting in and so was the craze to own a PC at home. Sharad realized that this was the opportunity he could not afford to miss. Equipped with his boyish charm, he moved in fast and spotted some potential (read powerful and influential) clients. He not only installed a machine in their homes, but also agreed to be their Internet teacher as well. Soon the word-of-mouth spread and within no time an entire neighbourhood was on his client list.

Some of these retail customers, who were also large institutional customers in their official capacity, helped him get bigger sales and service contracts in the institutional sector. That was the beginning, Sharad had made a mark for himself in an over-crowded market. Soon he started participating in big tenders and evolved as an established player in the market.

Over the years he has added a number of other businesses (Software/Hardware/Education) to his portfolio. Today he is owner of a Computer Training Institute – a learning center of an Open University, besides a sprawling computer sales and services business, with an army of engineers and technicians working under him.

Starting from a small store-room on the third floor of a commercial complex, today he owns an entire floor in the same building. However the most interesting thing about Sharad is that he still continues to work 14 to 15 hours a day and has not for a moment stopped looking for new openings. For he knows that his agility has been his only weapon for his success.

Incidentally the term AGILITY is often confused with Speed. But Agility is different from Speed. Where Speed is largely about moving rashly in a single direction, Agility is

about moving fast but at the same time in control of one's speed. This allows changing directions as per the need of the hour.

In business terms it means getting deep into action from the word go and at the same time keep looking for new and upcoming business openings and opportunities. These new openings could be in form of new businesses or new marketing concepts or new product/service ideas or even in terms of a new way of doing the same old thing. ('New' here means for you as entrepreneur. It might not necessarily mean 'Innovative'.)

To sum up the discussion, there are three ways successful entrepreneurs create an identity and get established in the market.

a. They position themselves to be the LEADER at all the times.
b. They position themselves to JOIN the leader.
c. They use their AGILITY to spot an opening in the existing order and then move-in fast.

So far so good, but we have till now discussed the case of only those people who take to entrepreneurship by choice. We haven't discussed the case of Accidental Entrepreneurs. So now let's discuss the case of Accidental Entrepreneurs, people who get forced into self-employment because of the prevailing personal circumstances.

A Blueprint for Accidental Entrepreneurs

Before we discuss the blueprint for accidental entrepreneurs, it is important to highlight—How the case of Accidental

Entrepreneurs might be different from that of otherwise normal by-choice entrepreneurs?

There are certain things that would be unique to Accidental Entrepreneurs.

- Accidental Entrepreneurs are most **unlikely** to have any innovative business idea. In fact there might be nothing unusual about their business plans. Most of the times their business ideas would be poor imitations of the success stories of other entrepreneurs.

- Secondly even if they have some revolutionary idea, they might not have the capability to convert it into a pragmatic business opportunity immediately.

- Further, they are likely to be short on money and might not be in a position to invest big amounts or to enter into partnership with some already established market player.

- Besides, they might lack necessary experience/expertise to manage a venture of too large a magnitude.

- Finally, accidental entrepreneurs are most unlikely to have the entrepreneurial mind-set, i.e. the ability to keep the show running no matter what may come. They are likely to be running low on morale and might have logged on to entrepreneurship just to escape the trauma of being called unemployed.

Let's analyse how such people can create an identity and eventually succeed in the market? Here's a simple blueprint.

1. Start Small (in real sense)
2. Set reasonable targets and Get deep into action
3. Focus on developing Capabilities

4. Be Agile and keep a count of the changes happening around
5. Don't lose faith and don't rush
6. Once you start feeling settled, plan to increase your business operations gradually.
7. In case the business you have chosen doesn't show potential of long term growth, gradually add new activities to your portfolio. In other words, develop small 'Strategic Business Units' (SBUs) around a core business.
8. Plan to increase your revenue gradually, either through bigger operations or through a matrix of assorted/aligned business activities.
9. Get deeper into action and network extensively.
10. Gradually drop the poor performing business activities from your portfolio and intensify your efforts over the better performing ones.

If you manage to survive this long, which should be within two to three year's time, it means you are now at par with anyone else in terms of entrepreneurial capabilities. At this stage, you would no more remain an 'Accidental Entrepreneur', but would have qualified yourself to be a 'Complete Entrepreneur', at par with anyone else in the business.

11. At this stage develop and define your Entrepreneurial Vision.
12. Gather your focus and identify suitable OPENINGS in congruence with your Vision.
13. The moment you spot one, move-in fast to:
Be a leader,

or

To be with a leader,

or

Simply stay there till you succeed.

Let me share with you an example from my vicinity. This is the story of two accidental entrepreneurs, working as partners, whom I have seen grow and get established over the last three years.

Vivek and Suresh Singh, two brothers now in their late twenties, form a classical case for accidental entrepreneurs. Both the brothers had been roaming around in search of a job, when someone suggested them to get self-employed. After some deliberation they started a retail counter for stationary products from a room in their home. For the initial few months they would have no customers except for a few neighbours, who would buy occasionally from them.

Then one day an idea struck them to increase their sale, that too without investing any money into the business. The next morning they loaded their scooter with the entire inventory and parked it a few yards away from a newly opened school located in the outskirts of the city. It was their mobile stationary shop positioned to cater to the emergency needs of their target customers – the school children!

That day onwards every morning from 7.00 AM to 8.00 AM, when the school started and again in the afternoon from 1.30 PM to 2.30 PM, when the school closed they would park their scooter at the same spot, with all stuff loaded. The business picked and the turnover increased. The mobile shop concept continued for a few months, until the authorities decided to allow a stationary shop within the school premises itself.

On hearing the news from one of their regular customers, the two brothers moved-in fast to grab the opportunity. They sacrificed the mobile shop and got into a permanent shop within the school premises. But all this could come only after some tough rounds of negotiations with the school authorities.

The two brothers have been running the same shop for nearly three years now. Interestingly their original contract was only for a period of six months, however they made sure, through their efficient conduct and service that it never got terminated. But that's not where the story ends!

A few months back, the two brothers sent me an invitation to attend the inauguration of their new books and gift shop in one of the upcoming commercial centres of the city. At the moment this new shop remains open only in the evenings and on the holidays, i.e. outside the school hours, but soon the brothers plan to keep it open all through the day. The journey seems to have just begun for them!

It's important to remember that getting established in the crowded market place is a joint-function of two variables:
a.   Resilience
b.   Innovation.

A proper combination of the two can lead any entrepreneur to success in his/her desired endeavour.

And finally...

In the free market economy, it is often said that the customer is the king. However I feel it is not the customer who is the king, because it is the entrepreneur with conviction, who is the real King! Think about it and get set to be the King.

This brings us to the end of this chapter, the first under the Implementation phase. Here we talked about how to create an identity and get established in the crowded marketplace. In the next chapter we discuss about another crucial aspect associated with the day-to-day running of the entrepreneurial venture – the short-term money management.

8

Staying in Cash

'Don't tell me where your priorities are. Show me where you spend your money and I'll tell you what they are.'

James W. Frick

In this chapter we discuss the following:
1. Staying in Cash – What does it mean?
2. Staying in Cash – Why is it necessary?
3. Ten tips for Staying in Cash

Staying in Cash – What does it mean?

Business operations involve flow of funds in two directions – Outflows and Inflows. The outflow of funds occurs at two primary levels:
1. One-time Start-up Expenses (Plant and Machinery, Office Space, Furniture and Fixtures, License Fee, etc.)

2. Recurring Operational Expenses (Raw Material, Supplies, Wages, Rent, Telephone Bills, Royalty, etc.)

While the cash inflow occurs primarily on account of:
a. Sales Revenue
b. Fresh Investment (only at some later stage)

One-time Start-up Expenses incurred at the time of commencing the venture get recouped only through accumulated profits over a period of time (the break-even period). However, Recurring Operational Expenses are the ones that have to be taken care of on a regular basis. It is here at this front, where the effectiveness of the entrepreneur's money management skills gets tested.

'Staying in Cash' means generating enough cash through Sales Revenue to take care of the Recurring Operational Expenses on a continued basis. To put it differently, 'Staying in Cash' means always having enough cash at our disposal to suffice for all our immediate and short-term financial needs. It is about keeping enough monetary resources to ensure smooth running of business operations on a day-to-day basis. Experts call it 'Working Capital Management'.

Staying in Cash – Why is it necessary?

Let's understand it with the help of a hypothetical yet simple example.

Suppose we start a retail outlet to sell a product 'X'. The cost price of product 'X' is Rs. 10 per unit in the wholesale market and it could be sold for Rs. 15 per unit in retail, thus allowing us a margin of Rs. 5 per unit. We start the business by purchasing ten units of 'X', amounting to Rs. 100. For the sake of simplicity let's presume that we have incurred no other start-up or operating expenses. Hence our total investment (expenditure) in starting the business is Rs. 100.

Now suppose, on Day One, we are able to sell seven units of 'X' – five units against cash and two on credit. Thus our total sales figure for the day would be Rs. 105. However the amount of cash in our cash-box would be only Rs. 75. (Rs. 15 × five units) The balance of Rs. 30 would get realized sometime in the future.

On the inventory front, at the end of the day, we would be left with only three units of product 'X' in our stock. Thus we would be required to replenish our stocks to continue the business on Day Two. This means going back to the wholesale market and buying more units of product 'X'. Now the question is – **Where do we get the money to buy more units of product 'X'?**

Of course, we use the proceeds from the cash sales of Day One. Thus we take Rs. 70 from our cash-box and buy seven new units of product 'X' to bring back the level of stocks to ten units. Please note – **In this case, although we haven't yet started making any cash profits, we could continue with doing business because we had enough cash to take care of our immediate business expenses.**

Let's continue with our analogy and presume that on Day Two of our business we are once again able to sell seven units of product 'X'. However, today we sell five units on credit while only two against cash, which means our collection from sales is only Rs. 30 for the day, despite having a total sale of Rs. 105 on paper.

Further we presume that none of our creditors of Day One pay us today. Now the total cash deposits with us in our cash-box at the end of Day Two would be Rs. 35 only (Rs. 5, surplus of Day One + Rs. 30, cash receipt of Day Two), while our inventory would have once again come down to three units.

What do we do now? Where do we find the funds to buy fresh units of product 'X'? We don't have enough cash to replenish our inventory back to ten, or even back to seven, which is our existing level of sales. All we can afford to buy at the moment are 3.5 units of product 'X', which is not sufficient to continue or grow the existing levels of our business operations. In other words, we have run short of cash!

At this stage we would have to choose one of the following four options:

   a. Infuse more funds through fresh investment into the business

   b. Borrow funds to keep the operations running

   c. Restructure our operations in wake of the emerged circumstances, and

   d. In worst case scenario – Close down the operations!

In technical terms its called **shortage of working capital**.

Scarcity of working capital is one of the primary reasons behind the failure of a large number of entrepreneurial ventures all across the globe. The entrepreneurs simply run out of cash to keep the operations going any further. Working Capital Management is a science as well as an art. Entrepreneurs who are able to understand this dynamics stand a far better chance of succeeding in the long run. The successful entrepreneurs are those people who never allow their total outflows exceed their total inflows. As a result they are able to keep the operations running and growing at all the times.

Thankfully, like everything else associated with the obsession called entrepreneurship, working capital management can also be learned. All that it demands is a little planning, some discipline and a strong desire to keep the show running despite all circumstantial bottlenecks.

Please remember that the biggest advantage of effective working capital management is that the venture can be kept running, even without making profits, provided we have at our disposal enough financial resources to take care of our immediate and short-term financial needs related to day-to-day running of business operations.

Ten tips for Staying in Cash

Here we discuss some practical tips to help Accidental Entrepreneurs develop an understanding about this aspect of their business and help them evolve as efficient money managers.

1. Prepare a Time Budget, which means:

- Ascertain the level of Cash Reserves
- Identify the potential Outflows
- Project the expected Inflows
- Match the timing of the Outflows in correlation with the Inflows

In other words, plan your operations in such a manner that your Inflows finance your Outflows, thus causing minimum disturbance to the level of Reserves. In financial terms this exercise is called Cash Budgeting.

2. Maintain Proper Accounts

Small businesses normally don't have too many complicated financial transactions that might require services of an expert accountant. Thus with a little training every entrepreneur can learn to maintain accounts relating to their business quite efficiently.

Business Accounting should not just be seen as another financial exercise. Instead it can actually help entrepreneurs take sensible and timely decisions. The books of accounts are always a storehouse of valuable information regarding several aspects of our business. This information can help us evolve as a more effective business planner and an efficient manager.

Use of accounting software has become highly prevalent over the last several years by businesses of all sizes. Most of the modern day accounting software come equipped with capabilities for generating different kind of reports and analysis. These tools could be useful in taking informed decisions for all categories of entrepreneurs, big as well as small.

3. Allow no unnecessary expenses: Make every penny count

Every penny you spend should be seen as an investment. Every penny you spend should be capable of bringing back appropriate tangible or intangible returns in times to come. Anything that does not qualify as an investment is a wasteful expenditure and should be avoided.

There are certain unavoidable expenses associated with every business. For example legal and statutory expenses, certain types of marketing and PR expenses, infrastructural expenses, etc. Such expenses should be kept to minimum. If possible, such expenses should be linked and merged with the corporate image building activities.

4. Control Credit Sales

Although your first preference should be to sell for cash, but that might not be possible in all cases. If that were the scenario with your business, then always remember.

- Never extend unlimited credit to anybody.
- Keep a record of your creditor's payment habits.
- Rank all your customers based on their payment habits and accordingly decide credit limit for each.
- Keep your exposure with the 'bad creditors' to bare minimum.

5. Never finance losses with borrowed money

In case of sustained losses, the best course of action is to restructure the operations on the internal front and re-plan the activities in wake of new realities.

For instance, in our example above, at the end of the Day Two it would be best for us to refurbish the inventory by three units (the amount we can afford) and subsequently, start the Day Three with a target to maximize the 'Cash Sales'. At the same time we must focus on realizing the proceeds of the credit sales made on Day One and Day Two.

Internal Restructuring is always a better and sensible solution compared to added borrowing or fresh investments.

As far as borrowings or investments are concerned, both should be done when the business is doing well and not when it is incurring losses.

6. Slowly pull out your money

Many authors propagate the concept of doing business with 'other-people's money' – what does it mean? Doing business with other-people's money doesn't mean snatching money from others or duping them of their wealth to run your business. Instead it simply means, using your cash inflows to suffice for your cash outflows and simultaneously depositing all additional inflows to the reserves.

For instance in our example, our proceeds from the cash sales on Day One were Rs. 75; out of which we used Rs. 70 to buy supplies for Day Two, while Rs. 5 was left in the reserves. Let's imagine we repeat the same amount of business thereafter for next nineteen days.

In that case, at the end of Day Twenty, we would have a total accumulated cash reserve worth Rs. 100. Now this amount happens to be same as our original investment in the business. This would mean that we have pulled out all our money from the business and Day Twentyone onwards we have started doing business with other people's money.

This is a very important concept, which a lot of entrepreneurs fail to understand and still more fail to execute. But those who are able to execute grow several folds.

Once again continuing with our analogy, please note that on Day Twentyone, we would have an extra Rs. 100 at our disposal. Now this additional amount we can use as fresh investment to scale-up the level of operations. Or we could use this amount to add more products to our portfolio. Or, with successful performance behind us, we could use this reserve as a security to raise (borrow) funds from the market (Banks, etc.) and plan still bigger operations and so on.

By pulling out our own money from the business we increase the number of possibilities open to us, because the process brings about a corresponding increase in the amount of resources available to us.

7. Manage Inventory as per your needs

How much stock should we store at any point of time?

The answer to the above question depends on the nature and needs of the business, the environment of operation, cost of stocks and demand for the product. Every entrepreneur must work out the optimum levels of inventory depending on the above parameters. Besides, as mentioned in earlier chapters also:

- Always prefer doing business with reliable suppliers.
- Never lay all your eggs in the same basket; maintain multiple sources of supply.
- In case reliable suppliers are a rare community in the industry, maintain adequate contingency stock.
- In the end, your objective should be to operate in a manner which optimizes your returns and offers best value to your customers.

8. Maintain a contingency fund for acute emergencies

Three rules regarding the above:

- Always maintain an emergency fund, but NEVER touch it!

- In case you have to use it – refurbish it at the earliest!
- Somehow if you are not able to refurbish it – review your business plan, IMMEDIATELY! Perhaps there's something terribly wrong happening out there.

9. Stay Informed about your Short-term Financing options

There are a number of short-term financing products offered by banks as well as financial institutions to help entrepreneurs cover their working capital requirements. For example Term Loans, Bill Discounting, Letter of Credit, Factoring, Overdraft Facility, etc. The key to successful usage of any of these options is knowledge.

One must know what these products are, how much they cost, what liabilities do they incur and what benefits do they allow. This is one field where ignorance can never be bliss, in fact could be rather fatal. However accurate, timely and up-to-date information could bring magical benefits! So stay informed!

Following the newly made provisions in the Union Budget 2002-03, several public sector banks have launched 'Laghu Udyami Credit Cards' (LUCC) for small entrepreneurs and artisans as a measure to simplify their short-term financial problems. (Contact your banker for details or search on the web)

10. Avoid excessive business

This is largely about when things are going GREAT!

Sometimes, in the heat of the moment entrepreneurs get carried away and commit themselves to more than what they are capable of handling. Such people eventually end up burning their fingers and losing their business.

Successful entrepreneurs firstly focus on developing capability and subsequently increase capacity to make a smooth transition to the higher platter. Excessive business is not only bad for the long-term financial health of any company, but could also hamper its reputation in the market. Unfulfilled commitments are not easy to get away with in the competitive market environment.*

The important thing to remember is that an enterprise can keep surviving for a reasonable period of time even without generating profits provided it doesn't run dry of cash needed to take care of its immediate and short-term business needs. Interestingly one of the best examples of this type of survival in recent times has been the famous online store **Amazon.com.**

Amazon.com began selling books online in 1995 and has since added toys, electronics, tools and other merchandise. The company has more than 25 million customers and its total sales amount over $ 500 million in a single quarter. Despite these heavy volumes the company has always been driving towards profitability, instead of generating pure profits. However, what has kept the company going has been some clever working capital management and planned capital management. The same could be applicable for your venture as well.

---

* For any detailed coverage on topics like Working Capital Management, Inventory Management and Cash Management, you could refer to the book *Finance Sense – An Easy guide for Non-Finance Executives* by Prasanna Chandra.

This brings us to the end of our discussion on money management. In our next chapter, the last under the Implementation phase, we talk about the relevance of networks in reference to entrepreneurial success.

9

Leading and Networking

'When we survey our lives and endeavors, we soon observe that almost the whole of our actions and desires are bound up with the existence of other human beings.'

Albert Einstein

In this chapter we discuss the following:
1. The Art of Networking
2. Building the Network
   a. Internal
   b. External
   c. Peripheral
3. The 'Priceless' Network – An Analogy

The Art of Networking

Some time ago, I was attending a lecture cum panel discussion. The topic was 'Relevance of the teachings of Ramayana in

Modern Management'. The session had some renowned management thinkers seated on the dais and the hall was packed to its capacity with professionals from diverse streams. As expected the discussion had gone intense from the very outset! There were views and opinions; examples and anecdotes; testimonials and theories; myths and stories all being quoted one after another. In the middle of the pow-wow someone asked, "What perhaps could be the greatest learning we as professional managers could imbibe from the life of Lord Rama?"

The answers started flowing in, first from the members on the dais and then from the audience. Those were all good answers, but the one that stole the show came from a young IT professional just two months into his first job. He said, "The most interesting thing we can learn from the life of Lord Rama is the Art of Networking, i.e. the art of bringing together people of diverse skills, intelligence, competence, beliefs and interests and lead them into a mission to achieve the desired goal."

Lord Rama definitely was a great networker, however, I feel an entrepreneur has to be an even better networker. I say this because the situation into which Lord Rama had been subjected was a 'win-lose' one. As a result he needed to network only on the internal front, i.e. build a strong and capable team that could take on the mighty Ravana and his majestic army.

In contrast, an entrepreneur has to be part of a 'win-win' game. Thus he/she must not only build a strong team by attracting the best talent (internal networking), but also build a bond of trust and reliability with their customers (external networking). Further the entrepreneur must collaborate with several other people to streamline their internal processes and deliver best value proposition to their customers. These people could be their suppliers, channel partners, advertising agency, service providers, vendors, etc. (peripheral networking).

In other words, every entrepreneurial venture, big as well as small, is a network of people, institutions and agencies working in coordination with each other to fulfill diverse objectives and achieve a 'win-win' proposition.

Building the Network

As mentioned earlier, there are three levels of networking associated with every entrepreneurial venture. These are:

1. **Internal Networking**, which includes networking amongst partners, co-workers, team-members, employees and associates, etc.
2. **External Networking**, which includes networking with the Customers – target as well as potential.
3. **Peripheral Networking**, which might include networking with people and agencies like Service providers, Suppliers, Channel partners and even Competitors.

The question at this stage is – How to build a progressive network? Although this is something more within the domains of practical application rather than theoretical descriptions, but still to answer the question, let's discuss some simple tips that could help accidental entrepreneurs network effectively over each of the above three fronts.

INTERNAL NETWORKING

Two Questions:

Question 1: What basic quality does an entrepreneur need to network cohesively on the internal front?

Answer: An ability to attract the best possible talent and get them associated with the venture as it grows.

Question 2: What makes a new venture attractive for talented people to join, other than of course the monetary benefits?

Answer:

1. A Favourable Brand Image
2. Challenging job profile
3. Conducive work environment
4. Promising growth opportunities
5. Good Governance

Based on the above, here's a small list of **dos** and **don'ts** that new entrepreneurs might find useful.

- Partner only with people with whom you can share a common vision and with whom you can work as a team.
- In case of employees – Hire Carefully and Hire the best possible talent.
- Be a good employer.
- Lead from the front and get your workforce involved with a high level of motivation.
- Generate a sense of belonging in your workforce.
- Please Remember: Money is not always the only motivational factor.
- Standardize internal processes to streamline operations.

- Don't punish failures indiscriminately.
- Encourage people to learn from their mistakes. Make them feel responsible.
- Don't give away... but never hesitate to distribute whenever appropriate!
- Never tolerate mediocrity at work.
- Denounce any indiscipline sternly.
- Throw-out any 'Problem Child' as soon as you spot one.

The better you handle your co-workers, the brighter the talent would be willing to work with you, and not always for the highest financial remuneration. If we look around at some of the most successful entrepreneurs, then we would find that these people have always chosen to work with the smartest and the best. So whether it is N.R. Narain Murthy of Infosys or Prannoy Roy of NDTV, the best have always preferred to associate themselves with the best and so should you!

EXTERNAL NETWORKING

Two Questions:

Question 1: What primary quality does an entrepreneur need to build a stout relationship with a large base of customers?

Answer: An ability to identify a few valuable customers and then utilize the goodwill to acquire new customers and retain them forever.

Question 2: What do customers look for, before opting to become valuable?

Answer:

1. Usefulness
2. Value for money
3. Affordability
4. Reliability
5. Respect

Based on the above, here's a small list of **dos** and **don'ts** that new entrepreneurs might find useful:

- Under Promise – Over Deliver!
- Listen More – Talk Less!
- Be Consistent in your Communication as well as in your Services
- Stay informed of their needs
- Never lose touch with your customers
- Keep watching the changing trends
- Change with the happening changes
- Keep identifying the most valuable customers. Treat them like King!
- Focus on generating repeat business
- Utilize the goodwill generated with the Most Valuable Customers to acquire New Customers
- Simultaneously, also identify the bad customers (Defaulters, Troublemakers, etc.)
- Reduce your exposure to this bunch, without being arrogant.

Media – The two way tool

In today's world Media plays a crucial role in the conduct of any business. On one hand if it holds the potential of helping us carry our message to the outside world, then on the other it provides an interface to let us know what's happening in the world outside. Here are a few simple tips for using media for optimum entrepreneurial performance. Out-bound Communication (Advertising, PR and Image building):

- Choose the media best suited to your kind of business. (Print Media, Digital Media, Outdoor Exhibitions, Trade Shows, Road Shows, Sponsored Events, Conferences, etc.)
- Please remember that the costliest or the glossiest might not always be the most effective.
- Get Innovative – Using mass media is all about grabbing attention of the target group. Hence it's important to make every penny count.
- Be consistent in your communication with the outside world over every platform.
- Deliver what you promise, both in content and spirit.

In-bound Communication (Market Research, Market Intelligence, Industry Information, etc.):

- Identify the sources of information relevant to your business, both at the micro as well as macro level. (Newspapers, Publications, Advertisements, Periodicals, Newsletters, Websites, TV/Radio shows, Exhibitions, Conferences, etc.)
- Stay informed about your industry through what gets published/displayed in the Media.
- Keep identifying opportunities for future expansion/ growth of business.

In the end, it is all about acquiring the right information for conveying the right message through the right channel to build the right image in the minds of the right customers. Simple, isn't it!

PERIPHERAL NETWORKING

Two Questions:

Question 1: What primary quality does an entrepreneur need to build a mutually beneficial association with the peripheral partners of the business?

Answer: An ability to identify reliable service providers and use their resources to keep the operations running smoothly and efficiently without incurring any excessive or wasteful expenditure.

Question 2: What do we as entrepreneurs expect from our peripheral partners?

Answer:
1. Reliability
2. Value for money
3. Affordability
4. Accessibility
5. Respect

In other words, same as that our customers expect from us. Here's a small list of **dos** and **don'ts** new entrepreneurs might find useful.

- Map all your needs and requirements in advance (Planning Phase – Chapter 5).

- Do business only with reliable people.
- Do business with people who show commitment to service.
- In case of constrained resources, learn to derive a trade-off between cost and quality.
- Remain vigilant to the happening changes.

We have already talked about managing the suppliers and channel partner relationship in our earlier chapters. Thus we would not dwell into those areas over here. However, here we shall discuss a few points about another peripheral partner, i.e. the Competitors.

Why do we need to network with Competitors?

At the outset for two reasons:

1. To make an industry level representation with the authorities/government
2. To share information of common interest and for synergy of ideas

Unfortunately it is more difficult to form such competitor level associations amongst small businesses than amongst the big ones, where there already exist a large number of industry associations, trade promotion bodies, etc. The sense of insecurity is perhaps the major reason that prevents small and medium sized entrepreneurs from sharing the platform with their contemporaries. However, wherever such associations exist and are being run with a positive frame of mind, they have proved beneficial for all.

Some interesting overseas examples include:

- **TiE – The Indus Entrepreneurs** (*www.tie.org*), an association of Indian entrepreneurs in Silicon Valley, with chapters in India as well.

- **Arab Forum for Young Entrepreneurs** (*www.afye.net*)
- **European Network of Forest Entrepreneurs** (*www.enfe.net*) &
- **Federation of Women Entrepreneurs of Malaysia**

This brings us to the end of our brief discussion on how to develop a sustainable network at internal, external and peripheral levels. However before we conclude the chapter, let's see how effective networking can transform even a very mundane idea into something par excellence. Let's discuss the story of development of a priceless network, which has since then attained global recognition and all this has been possible because the people running this venture have been great networkers.

The 'Priceless' Network – An Analogy

What does the word *'priceless'* translate into Sanskrit?

Amul

The Utterly Butterly Delicious – 'Amul' – one of the most respected brands of India presents a perfect case for how proper networking at the three fronts could lead even a small unknown venture to grow and attain global recognition.

What it is today?

The Gujarat Cooperative Milk Marketing Federation (GCMMF), which owns the 'Amul' brand, is a state level apex body of milk cooperatives in Gujarat. It has twelve district cooperative milk producers' unions as its members. These twelve unions comprise of 10852 village societies which collectively host 2.23 million individual milk producers.

The federation collects on an average 4.5 million litres of milk every day (6 million during winters) and its range of products include Pasteurized Milk, Butter, Cheese, Ice Cream, Ethnic Sweets, Pure Ghee, Milk Powder, Baby Food, Chocolate and Confectioneries, etc. The federation also markets Edible Oils under the brand name 'Dhara'. It's total annual sales turnover is over Rs. 23 billion (US $ 500 million).

It has dairy and milk processing facilities at three locations in Gujarat, besides having two separate plants for producing 1,450 metric tons of cattle feed per day. Over the years the federation has developed a state-of-art infrastructure for animal breeding. It has sixteen mobile Veterinary Dispensaries, besides first-aid veterinary services in almost all village societies. The federation also brings out a monthly newsletter in simple Gujarati for its members.

How had it started?

The story of 'Amul' dates back to 1946, when some farmers from Gujarat approached the Iron Man of India, Sardar Vallabhbhai Patel for help. Like any other village in India, these villagers were also largely dependent on seasonal crops for their survival. Whatever extra milk they produced from their cattle, had to be sold to the middlemen at almost a throwaway price.

These middlemen would further sell the same milk at high profits for consumption under Bombay Milk Scheme. When the farmers discovered the truth about the margins the middlemen would earn on their milk, they approached

Sardar Patel for help and advice. Sardar Patel suggested them to get united under a cooperative and take upon themselves the onus of processing and marketing their milk and dairy products.

It was by no means an easy task. In fact at the outset it looked practically an impossible idea. It was beyond anybody's imagination to assemble poor, oppressed and illiterate farmers and village folks under one umbrella and get them to see the vision behind such an idea. Moreover for running such a cooperative, there was a need for skilled people to handle administrative, managerial and technical responsibilities, which was nowhere present. Anyhow the vision had been floated and Sardar Patel had placed the responsibility of seeing it through on the shoulders of his trusted lieutenant Morarji Desai.

It was at this juncture that Tribhuvandas Patel, a local farmer, took upon himself the task of networking the farmers and milk producers. In the meanwhile Dr V. Kurien brought to the movement his managerial skills, while H.M. Dalaya pledged technical support to the project.

Working collectively, they managed to bring together farmers in two villages and convinced them to make village level cooperative society. These two cooperatives were united under a District level Union and thus was born the *Kaira District Cooperative Milk Producers' Union Limite,* at Anand, Gujarat. It was sometime here when the union adopted AMUL as the brand name for its products.

It was a humble beginning with just a few members and a total collection of 250 litres of milk a day. Soon the union started selling directly to the Bombay Milk Scheme and as the benefits of the cooperative became apparent, farmers in other villages also formed cooperatives and joined the movement... and the movement has not stopped growing even today!

How is it networked today?

On the **Internal Front** the movement operates on a three-tier structure. At the grassroots level are the village cooperative societies, where a milk producer becomes member by paying an entrance fee of Rs. 1 and buying at least one share worth Rs. 10. The members then elect a managing committee, which in turn elects a chairman, all honorary positions. Salaried persons are employed by the society for milk collection, milk testing, artificial insemination and administration.

The milk producers get paid in cash for the milk supplied to the village societies every morning and evening. The village societies in turn sell the milk to the District Union for a little profit, a part of which is distributed to the members every year as bonus.

The district level union is managed by a Board of Directors, 12 of whom are Chairpersons of various village societies. The Board of Directors elect a Managing Director who in turn is responsible for the running of Plants and the Union. Here also qualified salaried professionals handle all the production, distribution, quality control and marketing responsibilities.

In early years the Union itself looked after the marketing of the products. However as the number of Unions grew in 1974 an apex body was formed by the name of Gujarat Cooperative Milk Marketing Federation (GCMMF) to bring all marketing efforts under a single command. GCMMF is also an organization run by professionals and Dr V. Kurien has been its Chairman.

On the **external front**, 'Amul', which now rightfully claims to be 'The Taste of India', has been for years one of the most respected brands of the country. Further if you are an Indian and are reading this book, in most likelihood you would have been a customer of Amul sometime or the other. Hence I leave it for you to judge for yourself as to how the 'Amul' brand has gelled with you and your aspirations over the years.

Over the **peripheral front**, Amul is networked with countless number of people, agencies and institutions. It is beyond the scope of this book to describe the entire expanse, however I would illustrate two highly decorated nodes of Amul's peripheral network.

The first of the two is ASP, the advertising agency of Amul since 1966. ASP is credited to have created the famous Amul Girl – the small moppet in the dotted dress and her famous jingle – 'Utterly Butterly Delicious... Amul!' The same agency is credited with running the other famous outdoor campaign of one-line topicals over large hoardings since 1969 all across the country. Interestingly the 'Utterly Butterly Delicious' ad campaign of Amul is all set to enter the Guinness Book of World Records for being the longest running advertising campaign. The first advertisements featuring the little girl moppet in dotted dress had appeared in 1967. Over the years these campaigns have been instrumental in establishing Amul as 'The Taste of India'.

The second node of Amul's peripheral network, which I have chosen to discuss here, is IRMA (Institute of Rural

Management and Administration) at Anand. IRMA was established in 1979 largely due to the efforts of Dr Kurien in his capacity as the Chairman of National Dairy Development Board (NDDB). Dr Kurien had felt the need of professional managers in cooperative sector way back in mid 60's. Then he had approached The Tata Group to supply his company 'Amul' with some professionally trained managers. He also realized from his experience that the graduates produced by the Indian Institute of Management (IIMs) and other Universities would not fit the bill. Thus he resolved to create a world class Institute dedicated to the purpose and thus IRMA was established. Today IRMA sends out 80 managers every year and Amul remains one of the regular recruiters at the campus.

As far as this book is concerned, we have to conclude the Amul story here itself. However next time when you come across the Amul brand, just remember that it all had started way back in 1946 with a question in the mind of an ordinary farmer in a remote village of Gujarat. The farmer asked himself *"How do these middlemen make so much money out of the milk they buy from me? Why do I continue to suffer in misery?"* He took the question to others of his community and the network has since then not stopped expanding.

Interestingly, that is how it is for every entrepreneurial venture. Remember it all starts with a simple idea in somebody's mind followed by effective networking at all levels to finally deriving a win-win proposition for everybody. Hence conceive your idea and build your network. Who knows that in times to come you could be destined to join the league of immensely successful ventures like Amul, MRF, Wipro, Nirma or Reliance!

This brings us to the end of this chapter as well as to the end of our discussion under the 'Implementation Phase'. Over the three chapters in this section we talked about three essential aspects related to the start-up enterprises during the execution stage. Next we move on to the 'Audit Phase', where we discuss the issues related to the assessment of actual performance vis-à-vis what we had mapped while planning the venture.

SECTION IV

AUDIT PHASE

10

Excelling Entrepreneurs – Audit

'They keep moving the Cheese... Get ready for the cheese to move.'

Dr Spencer Johnson

This is the last section of the book and here we shall discuss how to conduct a comprehensive audit of our business venture and plan for the future. We shall discuss separately the case of entrepreneurs who might be excelling in their venture and those who might be struggling. This chapter is dedicated to the audit requirements of excelling entrepreneurs.

In this chapter we discuss the following:

1. Who's an Excelling Entrepreneur?
2. Excelling Entrepreneurs – Why conduct an Audit?
3. When to conduct an Audit?
4. The Questions to be asked
    a. Assessment of the past
    b. Planning for the future

Who's an Excelling Entrepreneur?

One who thinks he/she is! It is actually an intuitive feeling like being happy or being satisfied, which relates to a particular state of mind. We don't need a certificate from anyone to let us know if we are happy or satisfied because when we are, we simply know that we are! Similarly when our business is doing well, we would simply know that it's doing well.

Besides there would be other factors, like sufficient cash at our disposal, encouraging sales turnover, growing market penetration, expanding customer base, etc., all of which would convey a 'feel-good' message to us and would tell us automatically that, yes, we are on the right track.

Excelling Entrepreneurs – Why Conduct an Audit?

The question is:

Why conduct an Audit when we know that the things are going well?

The answer is, because:

a. Once successful doesn't mean always successful! Continued success demands uninterrupted assessment, planning and execution.

b. No one is unsinkable in the ocean, be it a small boat or a huge Titanic! An Audit is needed to identify any loopholes that might have unknowingly crept into the system. Besides an audit is needed to strengthen the 'growth engines' of the business.

c. No matter how well you plan, no matter how well you execute, some surprises are bound to occur! An Audit is necessary to understand the long-term impact of such unexpected development – positive as well as negative.

The history of entrepreneurship is full of examples where people have lost just after having made, what appeared to be a perfect start.

Some of the most scintillating examples of such failures come from the dot.com age. Definitely not all those dot.coms were mere crazy fantasies of over-enthusiastic young geeks. Some were indeed genuinely brilliant business ideas that had even gathered a good market base in a very short time (e.g. Jaldi.com, Entranceguru.com, Trade2Gain.com). Yet, these ventures got swept away with the tides of times for one reason or the other.

Excelling Entrepreneurs in past have shown to fail due to one or more of the following five reasons:

1. Over Opportunism
2. Excessive Business
3. Working Capital crisis
4. Loss of Customer focus
5. Internal Mismanagement

Besides the above there is another totally different aspect of the same problem. A large number of small-time 'quickly-successful' entrepreneurs, tend to get influenced by two things very quickly. These are:

1. Complacence
2. Fear of Failure

I am referring to the same syndrome, which Dr Spencer Johnson in his book, *'Who Moved My Cheese?'* has described so wonderfully. Self-satisfaction is an important attribute for happy existence, however often what gets mistaken for satisfaction is actually complacence. A large number of people, especially small time entrepreneurs, after having tasted a little success at the very outset, just try to hang on to it and stop trying for anything any further.

Fear of losing whatever little they have achieved and lack of self-confidence keeps them tied to the existing order. Such people land in big trouble the moment something unexpected brings a sudden change in the existing order. At that time such people get caught unawares.

The only way to avoid these mousetraps is to keep reviewing the business on a regular basis and hence conduct an Audit.

When to conduct an Audit?

The answer to this question goes back to the Planning Phase (Chapter 6).

'When had I planned to conduct a comprehensive Audit?'
- Was it after completion of a specific job or
- Was it after attainment of some definite objective or
- Was it after a particular span of time or
- Was it in correlation to the needs of my business or industry?

For example, a friend and fellow-entrepreneur, who is a tour operator, performs a comprehensive Audit every quarter, besides reviewing his strategy, just before and after every holiday and festive season.

To put it broadly, a comprehensive Audit should be performed at least once every year, otherwise as per the needs of your business or your personal preferences. And yes, it must be a written Audit!

The Questions to be asked

Once again, the list of questions supplied below is only indicative. Feel free to add more questions to the list as per your needs and circumstances. The entire process could be divided into two parts, viz., assessment of the past and planning for the future. Let's discuss each in detail:

Assessment of the past

What objectives/targets had I set for myself, for the period? (Chapter 6)
Targets in terms of:
- Business Objectives
- Sales Target
- Revenue Target
- Market Coverage, etc.

What have been my achievements?
What have been the primary reasons behind my success besides my own hard work and dedication?
What competitive advantage have I enjoyed to achieve this success?
Good quality of product/service
Clever pricing
Favourable market conditions
Monopoly market, etc.

How satisfied am I with my own performance as an entrepreneur?

Performance as:

- A Business Planner
- A Business Administrator
- A Marketing Manager
- A Customer Relations Manager
- A Finance Manager... and so on.

What was it that I could not achieve in this period? Why?

What things didn't go as per my plan? Why?

Would these failures matter in five years time?

If yes, how could I convert them into success?

If no, no problem at all!

Planning for the future

Would I continue to enjoy the same competitive advantage in times to come?

If yes, for how long and why?

If no, why?

What could be the expected threats to the existing order?

What's my plan to counter these threats?

What's my plan to re-create the competitive advantage I have enjoyed?

What could be the new opportunities coming my way?

How am I getting ready for these emerging opportunities?

What should be my target for the upcoming period? (Year, quarter, months, etc.)

Target in terms of:
- Business Objectives
- Sales Target
- Revenue Target
- Market Coverage, etc.

Would I be able to generate enough liquid cash to achieve these targets?

What extra inputs/resources would I need to achieve these new targets?

Resources in terms of:
- Money
- Technology
- Plant and Equipment
- Manpower
- Suppliers
- Infrastructure... and so on.

What's my plan to acquire each of these resources?

...And so on, till you have refurbished your original plan.

Handling Success is often far more difficult than handling Failure. Because when we fail, there is often a strong resolve to come back and try to convert failures into success. The options might not be clear at the outset, but due to constant thought and effort, we usually find some way forward. On the other hand, when we succeed, we are often left in a dilemma as to what should we be doing next. This dilemma occurs because we often fail to decide whether to continue with the existing formula, which has indeed yielded success or whether to hunt for a new formula. Very often we choose to stick with the same old formula, which had yielded success in past, and that's where often the problem starts.

In this regard, I recall an interesting conversation I once had with Dr Aditya Sahay, ex-CMD of Scooters India, the man who engineered the turnaround of the company from a sick public sector monolith into a profit making organization. This conversation had taken place just after Dr Sahay had retired from the company. Out of sheer curiosity, I just asked him, "Sir, after having achieved so much in your career, what do you plan to do next?"

"I plan to excel the excellence already achieved!" That is what Dr Sahay had to say for an answer. Somehow these words have since then become a guiding force for me. Thanks to Dr Sahay, for providing the mantra of managing success. Dr Sahay is now a Professor of Strategic Management at MDI Gurgaon.

This brings us to the end of this chapter, but before we close let's once again summarize the main points discussed in the chapter.

Three Points to Remember

1. Excelling Entrepreneurs must conduct an Audit because:
   a. Once successful doesn't mean always successful
   b. No one is unsinkable in the ocean, be it a small boat or a huge Titanic!
   c. No matter how well you plan, no matter how well you execute, some surprises are bound to occur!

2. The Audit should comprise two steps:
   a. Assessment of the past
   b. Planning for the future
3. In the end, if doing well in business, we must plan to excel the excellence already achieved.

With this we come to the end of this chapter. In our next chapter, we discuss how struggling entrepreneurs should conduct the Audit.

11

Struggling Entrepreneurs – Audit

'The question is not who could allow us but rather, who can stop us?'

A.P.J. Abdul Kalam

In the previous chapter we talked about audit requirements of entrepreneurs enjoying satisfactory performance in their business. In this chapter we shall talk about the auditing needs of entrepreneurs who might be finding it hard to make the two ends meet, i.e. the entrepreneurs who might be struggling to survive in their ventures.

In this chapter we discuss the following:
1. Assessing the Damage
2. Identifying the Options
   a. Planning a revival
   b. Implementing the contingency plan
   c. Exiting the business
3. Entrepreneurial Failures and We

4. The World's most unsuccessful entrepreneur

Assessing the Damage

Let's begin the series of questions once again.
If you feel your venture has not been doing as well, then ask yourself:

What objectives/targets had I set for myself? (Chapter 6)
- Business Objectives
- Sales Target
- Revenue Target
- Market Coverage, etc.

What has been the actual performance on each front?
What have been the primary reasons behind the respective short falls?

Were they external to the business? E.g.–
Changed business environment
Changed government policies (new taxes, new laws, etc.)
Entry of more resourceful competitors
Economic slowdown... etc.
OR,
Were they internal to the business? E.g.–
Mismanagement
Personal lack of ability
Wrong assessment of business prospects
Faulty planning
Over optimistic targets... etc.
OR,
A bit of both!

How can each of these problem areas be sorted out? What could be the best possible solution for me?

Can a revival be made?
If yes, How?
If no, Why?

At this stage we shall have three options before us. These would be:

1. Planning a revival
2. Implementing the contingency plan
3. Exiting the business

Please note that these three options are in order of the seriousness of the problems/shortcomings we might be facing in running our venture. If our problems were manageable we would plan for a revival. On the other hand, if we feel that it is difficult to plan a revival under the given set of circumstances, we could modify our business-model and implement the contingency plan. Otherwise, of course the ultimate choice of exiting the business is always there. Now let's discuss each of these options one at a time.

PLANNING A REVIVAL

Ask Yourself...

What things must I change in my existing business plan?

What should be my new targets? Targets in terms of:
- Business Objectives
- Sales Target
- Revenue Target
- Market Coverage, etc.

Do these targets actually look realistic and achievable? Why?

What were the things that didn't work in my previous plan?

What safeguards am I taking to avoid the same failures, this time?

What factors are going to help me achieve these targets?
    Internal Factors
    External Factors
How do I plan to utilize them to the best of my advantage?

What factors would offer resistance in achieving the above targets?
    Internal Factors
    External Factors
How do I plan to minimize their effect to the best of my advantage?

What new/additional resources do I need to achieve these targets?
    Personal (managerial/technical skills, etc.)
    Internal (more funds, new equipment, additional manpower, etc.)
    External (additional suppliers, channel partners, external partners, etc.)
What would be my USP?
Who would be my customers?
What would make my customers come to me this time?
How am I going to generate the competitive advantage?
How would the things be different this time?

What options would I have by the time of next audit, if,
> I succeed
> I fail

Please remember that in general most of the ventures start giving consistent returns only by the third year of its operation. On occasions when entrepreneurs decide to quit early, it is mostly due to their personal loss of belief in their dream. However, sometimes there are certain unavoidable circumstances, which force entrepreneurs to quit or redesign the business.

IMPLEMENTING THE CONTINGENCY PLAN

Ask Yourself:

What was my Contingency Plan? (Chapter 6)
Does it still sound relevant under existing circumstances?
> If yes, plan its Implementation.
> If no, what changes might make it work?
> AND, even if that doesn't work...
> What alternate plan/business could I venture into at this stage?

Sometimes under such stressed circumstances, it is quite possible that we might not be able to think of many suitable options instantaneously. Therefore it is advised that when facing such a dead end, we must take a break. Allow some rest to the stressed brain and come back some time later. Something shall definitely be waiting for us then!

EXITING THE BUSINESS

Exiting the business might involve a few complexities, which if not taken care of properly, might even further frustrate the entrepreneur.

Ask Yourself...

> What was my exit plan? (Chapter 6)
> What else do we need, in addition, to exit the business at this stage?

There is not much to be told on this front, however just two tips–

1. Get clear on all financial obligations before closing the business
2. Close down your bank accounts immediately thereafter

Please remember that the other legal/statutory requirements (cancellation of Sales Tax registration, etc.) might take longer time and effort to settle.

Entrepreneurial Failures and We

Till very recently failures in our country were strictly considered a taboo. Thankfully, with the changing social dynamics the mind-set is also slowly but surely shifting. Today, entrepreneurial failures are more acceptable than were say ten years ago. This can be seen from the fact that many unsuccessful entrepreneurs of the dot.com age have been able to find alternate employment once their ventures closed. In fact in some cases companies have preferred to hire only those people who have had their share of failures. The reason such companies offer is that what a single failure can teach a person in a moment, no amount of success can ever teach them in a whole lifetime.

Sabeer Bhatia, the man who had set the dot.com world on fire with his hotmail.com, once said during a television interview that he didn't learn that much from the success of hotmail.com as much the failure of arzoo.com taught him.

World's most unsuccessful entrepreneur

Here's an interesting story of an entrepreneur, whose career I feel could serve as an outstanding motivational example for struggling entrepreneurs.

In the year 1893, the chief engineer of the Edison Illuminating Company in Michigan USA, working from his wife's kitchen after office hours, designed a small internal combustion engine. Three years later he completed work on his first automobile, a two-cylinder-powered vehicle he called "Quadricycle". With financial support from a couple of prominent citizens of the town, this man resigned from his job and started a company by the name of Detroit Automobile Company.

Unfortunately the new company had no clear idea of what it wanted to do and thus had to be folded by the end of 1900. Out of job and desperate for an identity, this gentleman turned his attention towards an emerging sport called 'auto racing'. Very soon he proved himself to be quite a successful driver on the racetrack.

His popularity on the racetrack resulted in his establishing contacts with some rich and famous people. These associations subsequently resulted in formation of a company by his name.

Thus was formed 'The Henry Ford Company' in 1901. But once again differences struck-in amongst the board members and the man, whose name was 'Henry Ford', had to walk out of the company named after him.

To add insult to the injury, The Henry Ford Company, which was renamed Cadillac in honor of Antoine de la Mothe Cadillac, the founder of Detroit after Ford's exit, was eventually acquired by the then emerging conglomerate that came to be known as General Motors (GM). Although the connection has always been kept murky, it is said that Cadillac, one of the most well known products from the GM shed, was originally designed by Henry Ford working for 'The Henry Ford Motor Company'. Subsequently, Henry Leland, who had joined the company as its new chief engineer following Ford's departure, had carried the Cadillac project forward.

Once again jobless and frustrated, Henry Ford was in search of a dream and very soon he did find one. In those days, cars were expensive vehicles for the favoured few. Henry Ford decided to change the trend. He decided to make cars that the great American working class could afford. An idea, which had really few takers in those times! But Ford went ahead and formed 'The Ford Motor Company' in late 1902 and took control of his destiny. However success didn't come to him immediately even here.

His first product 'Model A' got him charged with patent violation, a case that Ford vigorously fought in the court and eventually won. 'Model A' was followed by a series of mid-sized, higher-priced vehicles, which didn't do too well in the market. Ford had to wait until October 1908 when his master creation 'Model T', a car priced at just $ 852 hit the American roads. Model T remained in production for the next 20 years, in which time the company sold more than 15,485,000 improved versions of the same car and simultaneously brought its price down to $ 260 per car. It was truly a car that the great American working class loved to possess and the Ford era had begun.

Moral of the story: Once Unsuccessful doesn't mean always Unsuccessful! Thus it's always worthwhile to give it a second shot. And perhaps that is the central message I would like my readers to remember from this chapter. So keep the faith and keep working, success would definitely come, if not today, surely tomorrow. After all you are in the game that involves working in obscurity and amidst uncertainty to see a dream come true... some day! Thus hold on to your dream to watch it come true... one day.

This brings us to the end of our discussion on how the struggling entrepreneurs should conduct an audit. In our next chapter, which happens to be the last of this book, we summarize whatever we have been discussing all through this book.

12

Summing up and Moving Ahead

'But what is beyond our imagination does exist, nevertheless.'

Mahatma Gandhi

In this concluding chapter, we discuss the following:
1. The Ten Commandments
2. The thing called luck!
3. Columbus – the sailor!

Ten Commandments

Let's summarize in ten simple memorable points, what we have discussed all through this book.

1. Choose a business, which you believe in and would love to run.
2. Start only when you feel reasonably comfortable to handle the challenge.
3. Define your business objectives in clear terms.

4. Design a plan to achieve these objectives.
5. Get deep into action from the outset.
6. Listen to your customers and keep looking for happening changes.
7. Aim either to be a leader or to be with a leader.
8. Manage your money wisely and observe strict monetary discipline.
9. Keep monitoring your progress on a regular basis.
10. Stay committed to succeed and nothing shall ever stop you!

And finally...

Albert Einstein, besides giving us so many things, also gave us three rules of work. They are:

1. Out of clutter, find simplicity.
2. From discord, find harmony.
3. In the middle of the difficulty lies opportunity.

Nothing can summarize the message I intended to convey through this book better than these three simple rules. Every Accidental Entrepreneur, like a small seed has a potential to grow into a big strong tree. In order to actualize this hidden potential all we need is some devout perseverance and a little self-directed performance. So have faith in your destiny and move ahead.

The Thing Called Luck!

What's luck got to do with success?

This is a very widely debated topic. The Motivational Gurus avoid it; the Spiritual Gurus profess it and yet the confusion prevails!

There is a group of people who believe that there's nothing like good-luck or bad-luck. These people feel that those who work hard succeed while those who don't simply fail. On the contrary, there is another school of thought that says everything is pre-destined, success comes only to those who have been carefully picked for it by someone unknown. In between these two extremes there is a vast majority of people who feel it's actually a mix of the two.

I don't know which of these three groups is correct, nor is it my intention to search, which of the three is more correct. Maybe there's something called luck or maybe there isn't, but then it doesn't matter.

Luck or no luck, it doesn't make a difference to the final outcome because of a simple truth that has prevailed throughout the world across all ages. This truth is that anyone who has ever tried to achieve anything in this world and has tried it real hard has sooner or later got it.

So if you believe that nothing can stop you from achieving your objectives, believe me nothing will! Instead Nature would quietly chose to conspire with you and create innovative solutions that would push you closer towards your objectives.

Perhaps it is this little mischief of Mother Nature, which those people who believe in luck, call luck! Maybe or maybe not, but then as I have said it simply doesn't make a difference!

Columbus – The Sailor!

In the 15th century, when it was widely believed that the earth is flat, there was born a man who believed that it was not! This man one-day set out to sail in the big ocean, equipped just with *faith* that the earth is round like a ball. He believed that this vast ocean is going to end at some place, where the land would emerge again and that land would be India! Christopher Columbus had set out to discover a new sea route to India.

There is a small Columbus in every entrepreneur. We all set out to sail into the unknown waters equipped with *faith* that we would reach our destination... some day.

As an entrepreneur, you might fail to find a new sea route to India but one thing for sure, you shall definitely come back discovering something that would make your journey worthwhile and memorable... just like Columbus!

So have Faith and set sail...

Bibliography

Rajan Chibba, *Starting a Successful Business – A Step Guide,* Penguin Books, 1999.

Debashish Chatterjee, *Light the Fire in Your Heart,* Full Circle, 2002.

Dan S Kennedy, *No Rules,* Magna Publishing Co. Ltd., 2000.

David Oates, *The Complete Entrepreneur,* Mercury Books, 1987.

Vivekananda His Call to the Nation – A Compilation, Advaita Ashram, 2001.

Ron Johnson, *The Perfect Business Plan,* Random House Business Books, 1993.

MK Gandhi, *MK Gandhi Interprets the Bhagvatgita,* Orient Paperbacks, 1980.

MK Gandhi, *The Story of My Experiments with Truth,* Navjivan Publishing House, 1927.

Dr Spencer Johnson, *Who moved my cheese?* Vermilion, 1999.

G Narayana, *Offering Love and Light,* published for private circulation, 2001.

Dr APJ Abdul Kalam, *Ignited Minds,* Penguin Books, 2002.

G Narayana, *The Responsible Leader*, Ahmedabad Management Association, 1991.

G Narayana, *Stable and Able*, Ahmedabad Management Association, 2002.

Debashish Chatterjee, *Leading Consciously*, Viva Books, 1998.

Prasanna Chandra, *Finance Sense – An easy guide for non-finance executives*, Tata McGraw-Hill, 1993.

Albert Einstein, *Ideas and Opinion*, Rupa & Co., 1979.

Richard Bach, *Illusions*, Pan Books, 1978.

Rabindranath Tagore, *Personality*, Rupa & Co., 2002.

Joel Kurtzman and Glenn Rifkin, *Radical E*, John Wiley and Sons Inc., 2001.

Koontz, O'Donnell and Weihrich, *Essentials of Management*, McGraw Hill, 1986.

Philip Kotler and Gary Armstrong, *Principles of Marketing*, Prentice Hall, 1994.

Articles of, Mahesh Murthy, in Businesss Today.

Websites

www.marketvoices.com
www.amul.com
www.cry.org
www.themuseumofautomobilehistory.com

Index